Life Is Worth Living

Second Series

Books by Bishop Sheen

Life Is Worth Living

SECOND SERIES

BY

THE MOST REVEREND

Fulton J. Sheen, Ph.D., D.D.

Agrégé en Philosophie de L'Université de Louvain
Auxiliary Bishop of New York
National Director, World Mission Society for
the Propagation of the Faith

ILLUSTRATIONS BY DIK BROWNE

McGraw-Hill Book Company, Inc.

NEW YORK   TORONTO   LONDON

Nihil obstat:
John M. A. Fearns, S.T.D., Censor Librorum

Imprimatur:
Francis Cardinal Spellman, Archbishop of New York
New York: Sept. 8, 1954

The nihil obstat and imprimatur are official declarations that a book or pamphlet is free of doctrinal or moral error. No implication is contained therein that those who have granted the nihil obstat and imprimatur agree with the contents, opinions, or statements expressed.

Dedication

AS A MOTHER DELIGHTS TO HEAR

HER CHILD'S HALF-UTTERED WORDS

SO MAY THE MOTHER OF CHRIST

TO WHOM THESE WORDS ARE DEDICATED

DEIGN TO GRANT THEM AUDIENCE

THAT THOSE WHO READ

MAY FIND THROUGH HER

THE SON WHO IS THE WORD

Contents

Preface

There are few things more humbling to one's ego than hearing a record of what one has spoken, or seeing a kinescope or a film of a television appearance. A thousand flaws appear and, with them, a thousand ways in which the same idea might have been made clearer or clothed in better raiment. John Ruskin offers this consolation to those who feel weighed down by their own inadequacies: "Imperfections have been divinely appointed, that the law of human life may be effort, and the law of human judgment mercy."

The latter statement is profoundly true; an audience is merciful. The failings of a speaker it takes to itself as symbols and signs of comradeship in human weakness. Such mercy, as Shakespeare put it, "blesseth him that gives and him that takes."

The contents of this book were never written out; they were either taken down from kinescope or else were recorded in shorthand during the telecast itself. They are scarred, there-

ix

fore, with the shortcomings of free speech. This does not mean to say that they were spoken without thought and meditation. As Pytheas once said of an *ex tempore* speech of Demosthenes: "His impromptus smell of the lamp." Molière made one of his characters bespeak the secret of what seemed like spontaneous utterance: "I'll make you an impromptu at my leisure."

The public acceptance of these telecasts has not been due to their intrinsic worth, but rather because they supplied a want. The public has deeper yearnings for Truth and Goodness than is generally suspected. Water is praised and is popular with those who are thirsty, but when the thirst is sated, it often demands good wine. May the written record of these telecasts into book form prompt others to give the same Truths which come from God in a manner more worthy of those who seek it.

FULTON J. SHEEN

Life Is Worth Living

Second Series

CHAPTER ONE

Three Degrees of Intimacy

Every human heart knows that there are various degrees of intimacy: some distant like an echo, others close enough to vibrate the soul. As regards audience contact there are three degrees of intimacy in our modern civilization—radio, television, and personal appearance, each one more friendly than the preceding one.

Radio is the first degree of intimacy, through the harnessing of sound to light. Sound does not travel very fast; in a certain temperature its speed is about the rate of 1,200 feet a second. But light travels about the rate of 186,000 miles a second. By amplifying sound and then dispatching it with the tremendous speed of light, one is able to talk in a few seconds to more people than St. Paul addressed in all of his missionary journeys.

But though one hears the voice of another over the radio, the listener is unable to return the speech nor is he ever able to talk back. This passivity on the part of the audience is compensated for by the amazing power in the human wrist, which can shut off any program it dislikes. Because one can never see the personality of the speaker, a speech must always be discreet and subdued; when one sees the smile on the face, one knows that certain words are not to be taken too seriously. When the eye does not see, the ear is apt to be more sensitive and critical.

Television adds the dimension of seeing to that of hearing, and thus satisfies one of the desires of human nature for increased intimacy. Many a soldier in camp boasts of the beauty of the one he loves, but almost always comes back the challenge of others: "But show us her picture." Television enables the audience to test the sincerity of the speaker by the manner in which he delivers his message. Due allowances must always be made, however, for the speaker on television inasmuch as those who sit in their homes little realize the multitudinous distractions there are before him such as cameras, sound booms, lights, engineers, technicians, directors, and stagehands—all of whom are hidden from the viewer at home. The test of sincerity, however, is somewhat lost if the speaker uses a teleprompter in which the message is unrolled before his eyes as he speaks. One way the audience at home can tell whether a speaker is using a teleprompter is to watch his eyes. They will always move from left to right, and back again, as if he were at a tennis match. When he reads from cards, then the eyes instead of moving from left to right always move up and down. Some who establish audience contact by television look better on the screen than off it. In my own case, a woman from Brooklyn, seeing me on the street, stopped and said, "You certainly look much better on television."

But beyond radio and television is the most intimate form of audience relationship, and that is personal appearance. Here there is not only a positive communion of personality with personality, but also an exchange of ideas which is the mark distinguishing man from beast. Some years ago, I had a man who was doing some work in the house where I lived and to whom I was giving much personal attention in order to save him from alcoholism. But every now and then he would take a "moral holiday" and revert to the bottle. On one occasion I said to him, "John McCormack, the singer, is coming to visit us." He was so delighted that, as time went on, the prospect of the coming personal appearance prompted him to impatience—"Three more weeks and I will see John McCormack," "Two more weeks and I will see John McCormack," "Three more days and I will see John McCormack." John McCormack finally came; and when this friend served the dinner, an untoward incident happened. Roast was served that particular night. Ordinarily, I do not remember what is served at the table, but as he brought in the roast, he got down on both knees and made a profound genuflection to John McCormack, as the roast waved perilously from side to side. All the while I was saying to myself, "I hope John McCormack does not think this is the way I trained him."

A short time afterward there was a terrific noise in the kitchen. He had upset the table and broken all the dishes, then began beating up the housekeeper. Shortly after he left the house. Three days later, he returned, saying, "Gee, I wish I could remember seeing John McCormack!"

Despite such disappointments the fact still remains that meeting a person and establishing communion with him far surpasses either hearing his voice on a radio or seeing his image on a screen.

Radio and television and personal appearance correspond to another trio of intimacies: hearing, seeing, and touching.

The first intimacy of the senses which corresponds to radio is the intimacy of hearing. We would never know that anyone loved us unless he told us so. Speech is the summation of a soul: all that it has been, all that it is, and all that it will ever be. As soon as we hear a person speak, we say of him, "He is a learned man," "He is a kind man," "He is a cruel man," "He is a humble man." Character is even revealed in the great books of the past, like those of Sophocles, Aristotle, Aquinas, Bonaventure, Bossuet. The first language of love, therefore, is that of speech in one, and hearing in another. Perhaps this intimacy is not used often enough. A Vermont farmer one night said to his wife while seated on the back porch, "Molly, I believe it is about forty years since I told you that I love you."

The next intimacy of love among the senses is vision. The heart is never satisfied merely at hearing the words of the beloved, or at reading his message. It wants to see the words born on human lips, see the earnestness of a visage, the flash of an eye, and the sincerity of character in the expression of the face. Communion between persons begins to be intense and vibrating the moment the image of the other is impressed on the mind and carved into the heart.

But there is still another intimacy—an intimacy so deep, so profound, and so personal that the greatest insult anyone can show us who knows us not, is to make use of it: that is the intimacy of touch. In the order of senses, touch is the high point of contact of personality with personality. That communion is regarded as such a privilege that it is often prefaced with the plea, "May I touch you?" A mother touching her child, a nurse touching the sick brow of her patient, a husband welcoming wife and a wife her husband—all these represent the crown of affection and the high point of fellow feeling of heart and heart.

If these three intimacies of hearing, seeing, and touching, which have their analogies in radio, television, and personal appearance, earmark the three intimacies of love, then should we not find them in God's dealings with men?

Should He not speak in order that there might be contact with humanity, and that men might know how much God loves him?

God has spoken! To find His speech we need but turn over

the pages of the Old Testament; there is written the speech of God. The Old Testament is something like radio: a speech without vision. But what discourse there is, for example, in those great commandments which were given to the Jews, and which have been the fabric of the world's civilization ever since:

1. I am the Lord thy God; thou shalt not have strange gods before Me.
2. Thou shalt not take the name of the Lord thy God in vain.
3. Remember thou keep holy the Lord's day.
4. Honor thy father and thy mother.
5. Thou shalt not kill.
6. Thou shalt not commit adultery.
7. Thou shalt not steal.
8. Thou shalt not bear false witness against thy neighbor.
9. Thou shalt not covet thy neighbor's wife.
10. Thou shalt not covet thy neighbor's goods.

There were other words too that He spoke:

"As the shepherd, when He finds his flock scattered all about him, goes looking for his sheep, so will I go looking for these sheep of mine, rescue them from all the nooks into which they have strayed when the darkness fell upon them."

And again:

"Come back and make trial of me. Then, the scarlet dye of your guilt will be snow white, the crimson stains will be like clean wool."

But love is not satisfied alone with hearing the speeches of the beloved; love also wants to see. If God is to sound another intimacy of love, He must not only speak to man; He must be seen. Vision must be added to revelation. This was done at the Incarnation of the Son of God in the Person of Jesus Christ. God was seen—seen in the form of a Babe in fulfillment of a prophecy seven hundred years old that His name would be called Emmanuel: "God with us." Men saw Him in a thousand other attitudes of love. They would have been embarrassed if they had had to pick the one in which Heaven's love seemed most intimate to men. They saw Him, for example, gather the children to Himself, press them to His Heart, and bless them. They saw Him pick up a child and place him in the midst of the Apostles as they were disputing among themselves as to who would be the greatest, saying:

"Unless you go back and become like little children you shall not enter the Kingdom of Heaven." This was another way of saying that no old people ever enter Heaven; by "old" people is meant those who lack the simplicity of the child which prepares for faith.

Childlike simplicity, or spiritual littleness and humility, is the condition of discovering anything great. That was why Francis Thompson told his friends in a poem, "Look for me in the nurseries of Heaven."

But though God's voice had been heard, and though God's person was seen and made visible in the human nature of Christ, there was still another intimacy which man had yet to explore if all the depths of love were to be sounded, and that is the intimacy of touch. Touched he was indeed when the woman came behind Him, saying, "If I but touch the hem of His garment, I shall be healed." Touched, too, He was by the woman who kissed His feet, poured ointment upon them, and then wiped away the tears with her hair. But the greatest of all touches was given by a man who doubted His Divinity. When the other disciples told Thomas, "We have seen the Lord," he said to them, "Until I have seen the mark of the nails on His Hands, until I have put my finger into the mark of the nails, and put my hand into His Side, you will never make me believe." Thomas was no mere doubter; flat dogged disbelief, and not hesitation, was his attitude. The very form in which he put his demand told that he was hugging his unbelief, and that he had no idea that what he asked for would ever be granted.

Later on the Lord appeared to Thomas, saying:

"Let Me have thy finger; see, here are My Hands. Let Me have thy hand; put it into My Side. Cease thy doubting, and believe."

Thomas answered, "Thou art my Lord and my God." Our Divine Lord then answered him:

"Thou hast learned to believe, Thomas, because thou hast seen Me. Blessed are those who have not seen, and yet have learned to believe."

Over and above the intimacy of vision; over and above the intimacy of touch there is the eye of faith and the response of the heart which is more reliable and more close than that which the eyes see and the finger feels.

There is nothing more that God can do to exhaust the intimacies of love. He has spoken; He has been seen; and He has been touched. To each and every person in the world He has given at least one of these intimacies. He is heard in His Scripture and by the invisible ear of the soul attentive to the whispering of His Grace. He is seen by the eyes of faith in the poor, and in His Body the Church, which is growing in age and grace and wisdom through the centuries. The final intimacy of all is that of touch reserved only for the chosen few who enjoy a communion with Him that is almost an interpenetration of the Divine and the Human, an embrace of love when He who is the Divine Host comes into the human heart as its Guest. It does not require much time to make us saints. It requires only much love.

CHAPTER TWO

Pax Sovietica

Every human heart ardently desires peace, but not everyone who talks peace really wants peace. In these days of Trojan
horses, infiltration, and violation of mutual nonaggression
treaties, it behooves us to study well what the Soviets mean by
peace. On September 12, 1951, *Pravda* pleaded for a "peaceful
coexistence" of the Soviets and the Western world. Incidentally, it is well to remember that there are two important Moscow newspapers: one called *Pravda* and the other, *Izvestia*.
One means *Truth* and the other, *News*. In Russia they say that
"there is no News in the Truth and no Truth in the News."

Are the Soviets to be believed when they talk of peace, or
"peaceful coexistence"?

The best definition of peace ever given came from the pen
of St. Augustine: "Peace is the tranquillity of order." It is not
tranquillity alone, for thieves can be tranquil in the possession
of their spoils; rather it is the tranquillity of order; order implies justice. Hence peace is the fruit of justice. There is peace
in a man when his senses are subject to reason, when his reason

is subject to faith, when his body is subject to his soul, his whole personality to God. There is peace in society when each man gives to his neighbor that which is his due in justice, and when society gives to its citizens that which is their due, and when all mankind gives glory to God.

What do the Soviets mean by peace? Peace to them means any condition or state of affairs of the world in which the Soviets are allowed to do whatever they please. For example, the Soviets invade Korea. Anyone who agrees with this invasion is peaceful; anyone who forestalls it or challenges it is in their language "a warmonger." Given this false definition of peace, it is easy to understand why the Soviets should contend at times that the United Nations is opposed to "peace"; this is because the U.N. frustrates Communist aims.

Peace, to the Communists is of two kinds: unjust peace and just peace. Unjust peace is any settlement or absence of war or violence which harms the Communist cause. A just peace is the allowance of military action on the part of the Soviets. Translating this into our language, a banker to the Soviets is "peaceful" when he allows the gangsters to take his money; he is against "peace" when he resists and calls the police. The terms are here so perverted that when the wolf attacks the sheep, the sheep becomes an "imperialist." The Soviet concept of peace reminds one of the man who importuned his friend, saying, "You say you are a lover of peace, Casey; then why did you throw the brick at Murphy?" Casey said, "Because he was very peaceful after I threw it."

As the Soviets have perverted the notion of peace, so they have also perverted the notion of war. The Soviets boast that they are opposed to war, but it must be remembered that they are not opposed to all *war*. Indeed, war to them is of two kinds:

Unjust war.
Just war.

An unjust war is any war which would help a non-Communist country. A just war is any war which serves the Soviet aims. Are the Communists, therefore, opposed to war? No, they are opposed only to "unjust wars," but they are not opposed to what they call "just wars." This explains why in the beginning of World War II the Nazi war against Poland was conceived as a "just war," whereas the Nazi war against Russia was conceived as an "unjust war."

In his speech to the Central Committee of the Communist party in July, 1928, Lenin, formulating the Communist policy of war, said:

It is sophistry to use the word violent when applying it to revolutionary action. This does not prevent socialists from being in favor of a revolutionary war.

This statement means that any war is right provided it helps the Soviet Revolution. The only wars that the Soviets oppose are what they call "imperialist" wars. An "imperialist" war to them is a counter-Soviet war and therefore counterrevolutionary. Even outside of war, Lenin said that violence is justified whenever it furthers revolutionary action. Violence is wrong when it is contrary to the Communist Revolution.

Returning now to the Soviet plea for "peaceful coexistence," what is the rational and sane mind to think of it? Obviously the Soviets are asking the world to accept their peaceful intentions, but the very words "peaceful coexistence" suggest some suspicion. When a young man takes a young lady out for an evening dinner, he never prefaces the date with "Let us have a peaceful coexistence this evening." A mother never pleads for "peaceful coexistence" with the babe in her arms. You go into a butcher shop, and, though the butcher has a cleaver in his hand, you do not shout, "Peaceful coexistence, butcher!" A husband returns from work; he finds his wife in the kitchen with a rolling pin in her hand—she is rolling a tart. There is nothing wrong with a rolling pin as long as it is below the shoulder. But suppose the rolling pin is above her head. Then he will have some reason to say, "Let us have a little peaceful coexistence." When a gunman attacks, you say, "Let us talk peace; put away your gun." No one ever talks of "peaceful coexistence" between Indiana and Illinois, or between Canada and the United States, or between the garageman and the car owner though the former has a monkey wrench in his hand. Does not their very plea for "peaceful coexistence" imply that they themselves are the villains? The term "peaceful coexistence" is used only when there is suspicion of the intent of another; for that reason one never hears the plea between members of a family at a dinner table.

How false the Soviet concept of "peaceful coexistence" is can be illustrated by this drawing.

The first of these five houses in the block is heated by gas; the second is heated by electricity. The third house we presently skip. The fourth house is heated by wood fires, and the fifth by coal. These different manners of heating homes correspond to the different economic and political methods among the nations. As the citizens do not agree on the method of heating a home, but nevertheless dwell in harmony and concord with one another, so different nations can have a genuine amity and peace one with another though they differ in methods of politics and economics.

Returning now to the third house. Suppose someone moves into the third house who is an arsonist. He believes in keeping his house heated by burning down all the other houses. There is, of course, always the danger of burning his own house, but arsonists never seem to suspect this trouble. The householders on either side never worried about the different systems of heating until the firebug moved in.

It happens that we have an arsonist in the United Nations. Just as American citizens would not sit down to a heating conference with a man who believed in heating his house by burning other houses, so we might ask if it is well for the United Nations to have among its members those who believe in setting fire to other nations. When an international arsonist pleads for "peaceful coexistence," saying, "Live and let live," we know from practice and from Communist theory that he means "Live and let me burn you." Our suspicions concerning this particular arsonist are deepened by the fact that he has already set fire in many other blocks of the city, and to allow him to sit at a heating conference is to miss entirely the point of both conference and heating.

Peace for the Soviets is, therefore, a tactic or a maneuver; for the Western world it is a goal and a destiny. "Peaceful coexistence" is a temporary relationship between the Soviets and the other countries of the world for the sake of the destruction of the world. Stalin once said that Russia is to be "transformed into the base" from which the world revolution is to be fomented. Peace, in other words, is to be exploited as an instrument for an aggressive policy.

This policy began in the summer of 1947, when the Soviets decided there was nothing to be gained from peaceful cooperation with the Western powers. In September, 1947, the Soviets began a "peace" campaign. In the announcement of the Cominform there was a statement to the effect that the world is divided into two camps: one is the Russian camp, the other is the imperialist camp. The Soviet aim, they declared, was to build up a strong façade of non-Communist peace lovers in order to further Soviet aims. The first move for fooling the world into believing that the Soviets wanted peace was taken at the "World Congress of Intellectuals" held in Poland, August, 1948. In 1949, a Soviet peace congress was held in Paris and Prague. All the meetings were arranged by the executive bureau, which was completely under Communist control. In October, 1949, a world peace committee under the Soviets took place in Rome. Guiding the policy was Lenin's statement:

We must be able to resort to all sorts of stratagems, maneuvers, illegal methods, evasions, and subterfuges so as to get into the trade unions, to remain in them, and to carry on Communist work with them at all costs.

The *Cominform Journal* of December 8, 1950, states:

All these peace activities are indissolubly linked with stepping up propaganda of Marxism, Leninism, and a tireless struggle against reactionary ideology.

The obvious aim of the Soviets was to enlist gullible lovers of false peace outside of Russia to help the Soviets in a military imperialism. The money contributed through these lovers of false peace helped carry on the war in China, as the Soviets bade the Chinese people in their "peace" campaigns:

To raise production and expand the donation campaign which has already provided 1,970 aircraft as well as guns and tanks.

The *New China News Agency*, June 25, 1952, stated that:

The Chinese peace campaign gave final figures to the arms donation campaign as five billion five hundred and sixty-five million people's dollars equivalent to the cost of 3,710 planes.

It is clear from the above that the Soviet desire for peace has no interest in real peace unless it be peace on Soviet terms, or *Pax Sovietica.*

The trickery and deceit of Soviet talk of "peaceful coexistence" can be illustrated by two boys preparing for a snowball fight. One boy represents the free world; he has his snowball fort and a good supply of snowballs. The other boy represents the Soviets. Not yet having amassed a sufficient number of snowballs, he says to the democratic boy, "This is a cold war, isn't it? Let's sit down and have a fireside chat by a bonfire." The democratic boy believes the other one to be sincere, and consents to having a bonfire built near his democratic fort. In a short time, the democratic boy sees that all his snowballs and fort are beginning to melt away. At that point, the Soviet boy starts the war. This is precisely what Russia intends to do: talk peace until it is ready for world revolution. Let America beware; the more we succumb to the Soviets' talk of peace, the closer we get to a new Pearl Harbor.

History should teach us that totalitarian dictators are never to be believed when they talk of "peaceful coexistence." At the

Nuremburg Rally in 1934, Hitler assured the world he wanted
peace:

In the sphere of foreign policy we have in the most solemn form
declared before the entire world the principles on which the German nation, without hatred or desire for vengeance against others,
seeks peace and friendship.

We have no more reason for believing that the Soviets in
their plea for "peaceful coexistence" are any more sincere than
were the Nazis in 1934, when they talked peace and then made
war in 1939. In every plea for peace by a dictator lurks the
threat of war. In the words of a character which Jackie Gleason
has created, "One of these days, Alice—one of these days—
powie!"

As a further evidence of the distrust we are to have in Soviet
talk of peace, recall the assurances that Molotov gave on
August 31, 1939, to Estonia, Latvia, Lithuania, in which he
promised the strict inviolability of the rights of these nations:

The special character of these pacts of mutual assistance in no
way implies any interference on the part of the Soviet Union in
the affairs of Estonia, Latvia, and Lithuania, as some foreign newspapers are trying to make out. On the contrary, these pacts of
mutual assistance strictly stipulate the inviolability of the sover-
eignty of the signatory states and the principle of non-interference
in each other's affairs. We stand for the scrupulous and punctilious
observance of the pacts on the basis of complete reciprocity and
we declare that all the spreading of nonsense about Sovietizing
the Baltic countries is only to the advantage of our common enemies, and of all Soviet provocateurs.

But now here are the facts of history. The Soviets annexed Estonia in 1940; annexed Latvia in 1940; annexed Lithuania in 1940. Let not America forget history, for history is memory and memory guides the present. The English never seem to remember history; the Irish never forget it; the Russians never admit it; the Japanese never make it; and the Americans never learn it.

The Soviets talk of peace for the same reason that Judas used the kiss. Judas knew there was something so Divine about that Saviour that His betrayal had to be prefaced by some mark of affection and token of peace, namely, the kiss. So the Soviets know there is something so sacred and so God-given in the liberty and in the freedom of democratic states that they can overthrow them only by some mark of affection, namely, the kiss of "peaceful coexistence."

Though the Soviets are not to be believed, Americans must not think that peace will be theirs simply because they have discovered the chicanery and trickery of the Communists. Our position today could be like the position of Jerusalem in the seventh century before Christ. A haughty and powerful nation, Babylon, was beginning to frighten and disturb the peace of Jerusalem.

Let the Babylonians stand for the Communists, Jerusalem and its culture and its people stand for the democratic nations of the world. As the more sober minds among the citizens of Jerusalem feared this belligerent power, a false prophet arose and said, "Fear not these Babylonians. They will not come in to destroy us. They are men of peace. Believe their word."

When the true prophet Jeremias heard this false prophet, he warned them that Jerusalem was in danger; that the Babylonians would come in and destroy the city unless it mended its ways. "God," he said, "is angry with us because we have not been following His law and leading a moral life." Quoting his Lord, Jeremias thundered, "Obstinately they have defied Me, the Lord says, Israel and Juda both; they disowned Me; Nay, they tell one another, this is none of His doing, harm shall never befall us, we shall have neither slaughter nor famine here."

Jeremias was so certain that because of the moral failure of his people the Babylonians would come in to destroy them that he symbolized the coming enslavement by wearing about his neck a wooden yoke. One day one of the false prophets who believed in "peaceful coexistence" with the Babylonians broke the wooden yoke on the neck of Jeremias. Jeremias went to God, Who now spoke through him concerning the false prophet Hananias: "Go and give Hananias this message from the Lord, wooden yoke break, iron yoke make. The Lord of Hosts, the God of Israel, tells thee that He is putting a yoke of iron on the necks of all the nations subjecting them to Nebuchadnezzar, king of Babylon."

Though the protestations of the Soviets that they are lovers of peace are as false as the promises of Hananias, America will be saved, not by merely knowing how wicked are its enemies, but rather by an inner regeneration of its spirit, a restoration of family life, and a return of the people to God. Then, if God is with us, who can be against us!

CHAPTER THREE

Children: Burdens or Joys

Some time ago we received a letter from a mother who named her baby Fulton. Fulton is now four years of age. One day the mother looked for him; she shouted and screamed, but no answer. Finally, the mother went to the garret; there she found the little boy dressed up, with coat, hat, and a suitcase in his hand.

She said, "Where are you going, Fulton?" He said, "I am going to New York to see Bishop Sheen. I was named after him." The mother asked, "What have you got in the suitcase?" He said, "My little sister. She is going, too."

That set us thinking about children. First how much trouble they are, and then how much joy they give.

One mother locked herself in the play pen; it was the only way she could ever get peace. A wife whose husband had a tendency to be alcoholic was always amused at night to see him get up and go in the kitchen for a bottle, but never take a drink. It was feeding time for the baby. Though he did not drink himself, he was still prepared to serve someone else a drink.

Ever notice how awkward men are at baptisms, or whenever they hold a baby? Just watch a man when a woman says to him, "Hold the baby, Bill." A man never knows what to do with the baby. His hands were never meant to hold a child. Somehow or other, his hands are like giant mechanical cranes. A child, to a man, is always in transit. He picks the child up and immediately looks around for some place to put it—anywhere to get it off his hands.

Men have various ways of holding a child. Some hold children like cocktail shakers: "To have and to hold." Others hold children like footballs: either they are looking for an opening to get rid of the baby, or else searching for a receiver to whom they can pass it. Still others regard children as a kind of mystery. They never know which end is which; and it is frustrating not to be able to tell top from bottom in a deluge of blankets: "I know it's in here *somewhere*."

But what a trial are the crying children! Ever notice how their eyes get smaller when they cry, and how their little noses almost become buttons? But the mouth! That is really tremendous! This subject of the crying child is a very sensitive point, because I believe that I was the original "Prince of Wails." I always hate to meet relatives and friends who knew me as a baby, because tradition has it—and tradition must be respected—that I cried for the first three years of my mortal life.

That is how I got the name Fulton. I was baptized Peter. I cried so much that I was a constant burden to my mother and father. To get a little relief, they used to take me to my grandparents, whose name was Fulton. I got to be known as "Fulton's baby"; later on the "baby"; and then the apostrophe was dropped, and I became just plain Fulton.

On the other hand, children are a blessing as well as a care, and among the blessings we mention three.

1. Children rescue love from boredom.
2. Children are the source of the resurrection of beauty and strength.
3. Children reveal the mystery of fatherhood and motherhood.

1. *Children rescue love from boredom.* Love can be boring; it can even beget ennui. When there are only two who love, love can degenerate into an exchange of egotisms, like two shipwrecked sailors on an island supporting themselves by taking in each other's laundry. Duality in love can be death.

For true affection there must be lover, beloved, and love. Hence lovers speak of "our love," as if there were something outside the sum of the love of both. They sometimes speak of it as something "bigger than ourselves," something that holds them together. It takes three to make love, and the third term in all love is God.

In marriage, the bond of love which holds father and mother together is the children. Children rescue love from boredom, prevent it from hitting bottom, and rescue it from the barrenness of epidermic contact.

How dull life would be if a musician were always picking up a violin and a bow, but never producing a melody; or a sculptor were always picking up a chisel, applying it to marble, but never creating a statue; or a poet were putting pen to paper, but never wrote a thoughtful line. Would not the farmer go mad if, each spring after he had planted the seed, he immediately dug it up, went on repeating the silly process, and never waited for fruits and harvests? What would happen to the mind and heart of a woman who, just as soon as the buds began to appear in her garden, cut each of them off, so that she never fondled a rose. Love, by its very nature, wants to bear some fruit; thus it saves itself from a duality that is death.

As the poet Davidson expressed it:

> Your cruelest pain is when you think of all
> The honied treasure of your body spent
> And no new life to show. O then you feel
> How people lift their hands against themselves
> And taste the bitterest of all punishment—

Of those whom pleasure isolates.
When darkness, silence and the sleeping world
Give vision scope, you lie awake and see
The pale, sad faces of the little ones
Who should have been your children, as they press
Their cheeks against your windows, looking in
With piteous wonder, homeless, famished babes
Denied your wombs and bosoms.

But when love escapes this deliberate frustration of the fruits of love, it loses a tiresomeness, because life has found its meaning. Love is then discovered to be, not like the serpent that crawls on the same level, but rather like a bird that has an ascension of love and begins to taste its sweetest moments in the higher summits of flight.

2. *The resurrection of beauty and strength.* People commonly believe that beauty and strength can be preserved indefinitely, thanks to creams, hormones, and permanents. The truth is that beauty and strength were given solely for purposes of allurement; hence they are at their peak when a family ought to begin to be founded.

Strength in a man is not an enduring quality; neither is beauty in a woman. There is something repellent to good taste to see men as they grow old try to appear young with "crew cuts," as if they were sophomores in college, thus manifesting an immaturity of spirit in trying to recapture a youth already gone. Women, too, with heavy rouge on cheeks that are sixty or seventy years old, also make but a foolish challenge to the passing of time. A beauty salon once carried the advertisement: "Water rusts pipes. What will it do to your face?"

Before marriage, the young man is admired for his strength, shown particularly by making end runs in a football game on Saturday afternoon. Not long after marriage when his wife asks him to take down the screens, strength seems to vanish as he asks, "What are you, a cripple?"

Beauty in its turn fades. Before marriage, the baby talk of the young woman is much admired and thought to be cute; but after marriage, it begins to get on the husband's nerves.

The conclusion to be drawn is, not that we are to be cynical concerning these endowments, but rather to see that though strength and beauty are not capable of being preserved through life, nevertheless they are capable of being passed on to another generation. When the child comes, then the father begins to revive in all of his strength in the child, as in the language of the poet: "From high heaven descends a worthier race of men." As the daughters are born, the wife begins to revive in all of her beauty, and the baby talk becomes cute all over again. The love of husband and wife becomes life's champion as it meets the challenge of death and, phoenixlike, rises from the ashes. Children then become as beads in the great rosary of love, chaining father and mother together in the sweetest slavery of all, which is the love of a family and the happiness of a home.

3. *Children reveal the mystery of fatherhood and motherhood.* Love is never satisfying when the heart feels that it has hit bottom. Where there are no more veils to be lifted, no more doors to be opened, no pages to be turned, nothing further to be disclosed, it is then that the heart seeks substitutes in vain.

As a melody cannot be produced by picking up a succession of violins and playing on each part of the tune, so neither can the happiness of married love be discovered by a succession of spouses. If there is to be happiness, there must be the deepening of a mystery, not the substitution of one experience for another. This is the function of the child.

The child makes the husband a father, and fatherhood is a shimmering refraction of the Divine Paternity from which all fatherhood and blessings come. From all eternity, the Eternal Father can say to His Eternal Son, "Thou art My Son; this day have I begotten Thee." The earthly father, reflecting that eternal act of generation, can boast that he has passed on the torch of life and prolonged the prayer "Our Father, Who art in Heaven" to "our father, who is in the home."

The child also makes the wife a mother. Man more commonly cooperates with nature, but a woman cooperates with God; she is the bearer of the gift of God to man. The word of woman is "Fiat," submission, surrender, cooperation with life. A woman's unhappiest moment is when she is unable to give; there is hell within when she refuses to give. Bearer of the cosmic plentitude, she fulfills her mission when she brings a child into the world. Looking down at that babe, a new paradox is revealed: it is the only time self can be loved without selfishness. A mother now loves a non-self in herself as her body becomes the ciborium of the new life, and her arms become its bearer as she passes on culture to ages yet unborn.

There are few transformations greater than that which the child effects in a home. The beginning of its presence creates in a man and a woman the powers and responsibilities of father-craft and mothercraft. God gives children to them as so much plastic clay which they are to mold with their own hands. In vain can they plead in juvenile courts, "I can do nothing with my child," for the judge and their own conscience might ask, "Have you ever done anything for him?" Whenever a child is born, a crown is made for that child in Heaven and woe to the parents if there is not a head for that crown! There is a story told of Leonardo da Vinci, who once painted the Christ Child. In later years, as he was doing the Last Supper, he looked for someone to represent Judas; searching through the streets and alleys, he found a dejected, miserable figure who posed for the traitor. But he was discovered to be the same one who posed for Christ. The child is not only the double of his parents; he is a concentration of love. He is also another person, a new center of liberty in the world. In each child, God whispers a new secret to the world, and it is the responsibility of the parents to see that the child keeps that secret.

Though the parents have generated the child and given it birth, there is yet another generation and another birth that awaits it: that birth is not from the womb of the flesh but from the womb of the Spirit. When the portals of the flesh were thrown open, the child became a son of man; when the portals of the baptismal font are thrown open, the child becomes an adopted son of God. Up until this new birth, the child is a creature; after the new birth, the child can call God in the strictest sense of the term, "Father," and he can also call one who brought the Son of God into the world, "Mother."

CHAPTER FOUR

Nurses and Doctors

Two of the noblest professions in the world are those of
the nurse and the doctor. Irvin S. Cobb once said, "A man
reaches middle age when he begins to exchange his emotions
for symptoms." This throws a particularly heavy burden upon
those who care for health; but modern conditions also add to
their trials, as is evident from this story. A little boy who
spent all of his free time listening to detective and crime stories
on television one day was afflicted with an earache. His mother
took him to a doctor, and the doctor asked, "Which ear is
aching, Sonny?" The young boy answered, "That's for you
to find out; I'm no stool pigeon."

First, we shall enumerate the three conditions for being
a good nurse and then the spiritual and moral requirements for
being a good doctor.

Every nurse should have three things:

1. An incision.
2. Cheerfulness.
3. A sense of the invisible.

She should have an incision in order that she may properly appreciate pain. It is not essential that every nurse have a physical incision; a mental incision will do just as well, if she has an appreciation of the suffering of others. Otherwise, there is a want of sympathy. It is easy enough to communicate ideas, for example, the idea that two and two make four. But it is impossible to communicate a toothache. If one is to know a toothache, one must have it. Such a person can say, "I know how much you are suffering, and my heart goes out to you." This identification with the pain of others not only prevents the heart from becoming hard, but rather lessens the agony of others by sharing it.

There is a world of difference between pity and compassion. Pity is an aristocratic virtue; it looks down on the suffering of others. Compassion is the democratic virtue; it shares suffering and pain and feels it as its own. The incision thus rescues the nurse from professional coolness, stamps her with that virtue of sympathy which is never wasted unless it is given to self. Such a nurse will never make a distinction between operations, defining a major operation as the incision which she has and a minor operation as the incision of someone else.

The second characteristic of a good nurse will be cheerfulness. There is nothing that so much contributes to the longevity of sickness as the long face of a nurse. A smile is laughter's whisper and has its roots in the soul. A patient feels a revulsion when a nurse enters the room with a needle as if she were looking for a target, but feels the infection of joy when entrance is made with a smile. Because the nurses have

to do so many unpleasant things, it is very important for them
to be cheerful, particularly when they wake up patients at 5:30
in the morning to ask them if they slept well—a greeting which
is generally a preface to having the face washed.

Tolstoy tells the story of a shoemaker who, returning home
one night, found a poor-clad stranger at a church door. When
he took the man home, his wife met him with complaint. As
she multiplied unkindness, the stranger grew smaller and
smaller. At every cruel word, his face wrinkled, but when she
gave him food, he grew more and more beautiful. The explanation that Tolstoy gave was that the stranger was an angel who
had fallen from Heaven and therefore could not live except in
an atmosphere of kindness and love. Only in such an atmosphere of cheerfulness do patients thrive.

The third characteristic of a nurse is the sense of the invisible, which means that every patient should not be seen
as something opaque, but rather as something transparent.

From a religious point of view, there is no such thing as a sick patient in Room 204. Our Divine Lord said that when He would come to judge the world on the last day, He would say, "I was sick and you visited Me; I was hungry and you gave Me to eat; I was thirsty and you gave Me to drink." The good nurses who are saved will ask, "When? When did we see You hungry and give You to eat? When thirsty, did we give You to drink? When sick, did we visit You?" And He will say, "When you did it to the least of these My brethren, you did it unto Me."

Every fevered brow will be seen crowned with thorns; every aching hand will seem to the nurse to bear the imprint of nails; every wounded foot will appear as riven with steel; and every aching heart will be one that knew the unkind kiss of a lance.

Nurses who serve each patient as though he were their Christ will understand the original meaning of the Red Cross. Its origin is traceable to St. Camillus, born in 1515 of noble parents. Before his birth, his mother had a dream in which she saw her baby with a red cross on his breast followed by a troop of children. He founded a community that he called "Ministers of the Sick" and chose as the emblem of that community the red cross, because it was a military sign of the Crusades; because Constantine after his great victory founded an order of knighthood called "Christian Order of the Red Cross"; because those who heal the wounded were to do it in Christ's Name; and, finally, because the cross on the breast was to remind one of the mortifications and the death of Christ. When

St. Camillus was shocked by professional cruelness and met opposition against his Red Cross, Our Divine Lord finally spoke to him, saying, "Fear not, oh coward! I will help thee, for it is My work, not thine." The Red Cross, therefore, stands for sacrifice and love such as were manifested by the Saviour for the sick humanity of the world.

Doctors in the nobility of their profession will be characterized by:

1. Reverence for personality.
2. Personalized rather than socialized medicine.

Reverence for personality. There is a world of difference between personality and individuality. A piece of chalk is individual, not personal. When you go to the grocery store to buy oranges, you may say to the grocer, "This is a bad one. Give me another." When a tube burns out in your television set, you buy another. In other words, individuals are replaceable. Persons are not. No one can take the place of another. Individuals are only means to an end. For example, one can use many hammers in making a brass bowl. Persons are ends in themselves, first of all because the soul of each person was created by God; because the soul is worth more than all visible creation—"What doth it profit a man if he gain the whole world and lose his soul?"; because every soul has been redeemed by the precious Blood of Our Divine Lord; and, finally, because every body is a tabernacle or temple of the soul and when that soul has been elevated to a higher order, God takes up His dwelling within through His grace.

Hence doctors will avoid two errors: first, that of considering man as a beast, as though he had only a body; and, second, considering man purely as psychic, thinking he has only a mind. The two are in close and inseparable relationship one with the other, as is proved by the fact that a man is the only creature in the visible order who knows himself to be miserable. Because the medical profession deals with God's noblest creatures, the doctor will seek to diminish as far as is possible the effects and the heritages of sin, which are pain and disease.

Above all he will be opposed to what is mistakenly called "mercy killing" but which in reality is "merciless killing." Merciful killing is a contradiction. It is like speaking of a painless toothache, a benign assault, romantic rape, honest robbery, hilarious income tax. Merciless killing is suicide with murder; a combination of the crimes of Judas and Cain, the two greatest crimes in the history of the world, despair and hate. The assumption behind it is that suffering and happiness are mutually exclusive, which is not true. One of the happiest women that I ever met in my life was in a leper colony I visited in the Caribbean. Noticing a radiant joy coming from her body already devastated by this disease, I remarked on her apparent joy, and she answered, "It is real; I am the happiest woman in the world."

Human life is not valueless because it cannot give material help to others. It is still capable of inspiring sympathy and love and service. How many husbands there are in the world with sick wives, and mothers with sick children, who in their dedicated love would not surrender their service for an hour!

In 1936, Hitler introduced the idea of merciless killing under the soothing but lying title of "Charitable Foundation for Institutional Care." The basic principle was that those who could not be of benefit to society should be killed. Up to the outbreak of the war, 275,000 people were put to death. Once the door was opened for destroying the sanctity of a single personality, there was nothing to stop slaughter. When Hitler called it "merciful," he did not define those to whom mercy was to be extended, unless it be the state. But once the idea is introduced that one may take the life of a person because he is not useful to the state, then it will not be long before we are taking his life because his ideas are not the same as those of the state.

Would those who believe in such an evil philosophy say that all idiots should be killed with butcher knives? Their immediate response would be, "That is not a 'merciful' way to do it." Were, then, the gas chambers of the Nazis merciful? No one who believes in this kind of killing would apply a butcher knife to an idiot. He wants that type of killing legalized so that it will not be the "I," but "they," or the law, who is responsible. The very search for legality is in itself a recognition of the crime of murder, which one seeks to escape by throwing the burdens on the anonymous or the state. Such men with criminal intent think that by making the handle of the knife long enough, or by putting it into the hands of the state, they will make murder legal.

Have they forgotten the Divine Commandment, "Thou

shalt not kill"? Are they unmindful of the oath of Hippocrates, which they took on graduating from medical school?

"I will use treatment to help the sick according to my ability and judgment, but never with a view to injury and wrongdoing.

"Neither will I administer a poison to anybody when asked to do so, nor will I suggest such a course.

"Similarly I will not give to a woman a means to cause abortion, but I will keep pure and holy both my life and my art.

"I will not use the knife not even verily on sufferers from stone, but I will give place to such as are craftsmen therein.

"Whatsoever house I enter, I will enter to help the sick and I will abstain from all intentional wrongdoing and harm, especially from abusing the bodies of man or woman, bond or free.

"And whatsoever I shall see or hear in the course of my profession, as well as outside my profession in my intercourse with men, if it be what should not be published abroad, I will never divulge, holding such things to be holy secrets.

"Now if I carry out this oath and break it not, may I gain forever a reputation among all men for my life and for my art; but if I transgress it and forswear myself, may the opposite befall me."

Finally a good doctor will give personalized service to his patients in contradiction to socialized service.

Many professions which were once dedicated to the person are now specializing on society. Social work is one field in

which this transition is unfortunately taking place. To understand why medicine should be personalized, one must recall
the important distinction between nature and humanity. Nature is concerned only with the species. Individuals may perish
by the millions, but nature is indifferent so long as the species
keep their pattern. Humanity, however, is concerned with
persons, not with species, and each person has sovereign, inalienable rights, and is just as important as any other person
in the world.

Three totalitarian systems have emphasized the importance
of species rather than personality: The Nazis absorbed the
person into the race. Fascism absorbed the person into the state.
Communism absorbed the person into a class. It follows from
this that only social health matters, but not personal health.

This is to forget that social health is dependent upon individual health; when, therefore, a doctor subordinates a person
to the abstract claims of the state, he is betraying his calling. The
good doctor will not allow his theoretical love for "humanity"
to become an excuse for not serving this particular human
being, whatever be his social relationships. Democracy is
grounded on the value of each person, and only those doctors
help to maintain democracy who serve first the person rather
than a class, a race, or a state.

The Patron of Doctors is St. Luke, who wrote the Third
Gospel and who himself was a physician. He it is who quotes
the words of Our Lord: "He sent out His Apostles to preach
and to heal." That is why Luke, whom St. Paul calls "our most
dear physician," does not use the same word for needle that

is used in Greek by the other evangelists. The others used the word *rhaphis*. Luke, however, uses the word *beloné*, which means a surgical needle. It is the same word that was used by Galen the physician in the year A.D. 130.

The clergy and the doctors, ministry and medicine, preaching and healing, are the two great professions which today are caring for persons and therefore preserving democracy. The two are joined together because both of them deal with that which is sacred, namely, the human person. May these two professions continue to be comrades and brothers in the holiest and loveliest service of humanity for the health of body and for peace of soul!

CHAPTER FIVE

Liberal or Reactionary

There are styles in ideas as well as styles in clothes; as some are snobbish about the latest fashion in wearing apparel, so others are snobbish about the lastest fashion in ideas. An assumption is abroad that anything that is modern is necessarily the best; this, in its turn, is founded on the assumption that progress in the world is inevitable and necessary, wherefore any philosophy which is popular today must necessarily be wiser than any philosophy of a hundred years ago.

This snobbery of time cannot be justified, because time does not necessarily make everything better; time could conceivably make things worse. For example, a white fence does not become whiter with time; it becomes blacker. Very often, what people call modern is nothing but an old error with a new label. It is very good practice whenever one is absolutely sure that he has a brand new idea, and that no one ever thought of it before, to go back and see how the Greeks put it. Some things are "new" to people only because they do not know what is old. It is conceivable that the best ideas may be those that resist the moods and fashions of the time: dead bodies float downstream; it is only live bodies that go against the current.

This snobbery of time manifests itself particularly in the tendency to class everyone as what is called a liberal or a reactionary, or to judge everyone by whether he belongs to the "right" or the "left."

It is our present purpose to show that one need not belong to either, because they represent extremes. These concepts of "right" and "left" are based on the idea of change. It is important to remember that, in everything that changes, there must be something that is changeless. For example, you meet someone whom you have not seen in twenty years, and you say, "My, how you have changed! How fat you have gotten." It may be very true that this person is a "victim of circumference," but how would you know that there had been a change in the person, unless there was also something change-

less about the person? The same person had to endure through the change.

Take another example: One woman meets another, and she says, "I liked you much better as a blonde than as a brunette," then with some degree of sarcasm adds, "But as a blonde you always had such fine black roots." If the person had changed, one would never know that there was a change in the color of the hair.

The liberal emphasizes change, the reactionary emphasizes the changeless. A reactionary may be described as a man with two feet in a pair of shoes but he absolutely refuses to walk. A liberal has been very well described as one who has both feet firmly planted in mid-air.

A reactionary has a son; the boy wears a green hat at the age of two. The reactionary father says, "Johnny, you wear a green hat now, you will wear it at twelve, you will wear it at twenty, you will wear it all your life." The liberal is one who says, "Let's give Johnny a new head—not a new hat, but a new head."

A reactionary is a flat tire to the wheels of progress; a liberal is the automobile without a steering gear. He does not know where he is going, but he is certainly on his way.

The liberal emphasizes the pendulum without the clock; the reactionary, the clock without the pendulum. There would be much less acrimony in the dispute between liberals and re-actionaries if the historical law were clearly understood that *every liberal is a reactionary;* he is in reaction to the last form of liberalism.

This can be illustrated by a woman who buys a new gown which may be described as "daring," "shocking," and the *dernier cri*. She causes a sensation at the ball the first time she wears the dress. If there is another ball the following week, will she wear that same gown? She would rather die first. She is already in reaction to the last form of liberalism.

A modern woman, from a liberal point of view, is described as one who drinks cocktails, smokes cigarettes, and has her fingernails painted bright red. Dorothy Parker, referring to the latter, says, "She looks as if she had just gored an ox." But this liberal in womanhood is in reaction to the last form of liberal, who was the Victorian woman: a teetotaler, wearing a tight collar, loving languid waltz tunes, and keeping an album of quotations from Lord Byron. This Victorian woman, who was liberal in her time, was actually in reaction to the preceding liberal, who was a Puritan who thought that the waltz was a kind of orgy.

In politics, too, every liberal is in reaction to the last form of liberalism. The liberal of the nineteenth century, whose ideas were made by Adam Smith and John Stuart Mill, believed that there should be economic production without state control. The modern liberal, who is in reaction to that old form of liberalism, believes that there should be economic production with state control, even with a form of socialism. The old liberal wanted freedom of the press within the framework of law; the new liberal, who is in reaction to that old form of liberalism, wants freedom of the press without the framework of law. In the domain of science, the old liberal believed in the determinism of the laws of nature; the new liberal believes in the indeterminacy of the law of nature. Every liberal is in revolt against the last revolt. The liberal of today is the reactionary of tomorrow, as everything is decided on the basis of time instead of on the basis of reason. Mules and jackasses have the choice only of going to the right or to the left; man has the higher alternative of going up or down, and that depends upon the way he uses his reason.

To restore sanity to the world, three conditions are imperative:

1. People must not feel but think, that is, use their reason.
2. In every discussion and presentation, it is always well to know both sides of the question and to decide them not on the basis of prejudice, but of reason.
3. Argue from the opponent's premises, not only from your own.

We know someone who fulfilled these three ideals. When he was born, his father went out and said to his neighbors, commenting on the size of the child that was just born to him, "Well, the little calf has come." Years later when in school, his fellow students noting both his timidity and his big legs, neck, and body, labeled him the "dumb ox." His very learned professor defended the youth, prophesying, "Some day the bellowings of that ox will be heard around the world." That intellectual giant born in 1224, whose name is Thomas Aquinas, wrote thirty-four volumes in quarto in Latin, some of which have been translated into English. His works represent the greatest masterpiece in the realm of philosophy. His gigantic powers of intellect naturally led him to God, and his parents and relatives tried to deflect him from his religious vocation. Being rather "modern," they thought the best way to do it was to develop in him an interest in sex. They introduced a woman into his room when he was studying. Seizing a blazing poker from the fire, he chased her from the room, and then traced upon the door a blazing cross.

The suppression of carnal instincts seemed to intensify his powers of mind as reason came out of him like molten lava. His first principle was: You cannot begin religion with faith; there must be a reason for faith and a motive for belief. This was rather astounding to those who believed that religion, particularly supernatural religion, was without a foundation in either reason or history. One of his friends, Raymond of Pinafort, who had been a missionary among the Moslems, was quite unsuccessful in disputation with his adversaries. He asked Aquinas to write him a book that could be used against the unbelievers. Thomas wrote in answer to that request his *Contra Gentiles*. He began it by saying that, when arguing with the Moslems or pagans, it does no good to quote the Bible or the decisions of the Church. When you argue with a Jew, it is all right to use the Old Testament since he believes in the Old Testament; when you argue with fellow Christians, it is right to use the New Testament; but when discussion centers on those who are without faith, one must rely on the one power and capacity which is common to all men, namely, human reason.

A second basic principle was always to give both sides of the question. This demanded a fair and honest presentation of the other man's point of view. One of his greatest works, called the *Summa Theologica*, gave mankind its greatest lesson in controversy. Discussing thousands of problems such as memory, passions, mind, prudence, temperance, the effect of carnal excesses on thought, humanism, the desire for God, he follows throughout all the volumes exactly the same structure: (1) he first gives the position and the arguments of the adversary; (2) he gives the reasons for his own position; (3) he then answers by reason the arguments of the adversary.

Take, for example, the problem of the existence of God. Contending that the existence of God is not self-evident, but must be proved by reason, he proceeds to ask if there is a God. He begins by giving the atheistic position honestly and fairly. The first argument he gives for atheism runs something like this: If God exists, He would have to be Goodness; but if He is perfectly Good, there could be no evil in the world. But there is evil in the world; therefore, God does not exist.

The second argument of the atheist which he considers is that nature explains everything; the scientific description of the universe being total, there is no necessity of invoking a Power outside of the world to explain it.

After stating the objections against the existence of God, St. Thomas then proceeds to give five very solid arguments for His existence, the first of which is drawn from the facts of evolution. Evolution to him is not only cosmic and biological; it even embraces the development and the unfolding of thought. After elaborating the five arguments for the existence of God, he then answers the atheistic objections which he considered at the beginning.

How different are the so-called thinkers of today. Pick up a volume of Karl Marx, the philosopher of Communism, and there will not be found any consideration of the other man's point of view, such as the argument for private property or for the existence of God. In the writings of St. Thomas, arguments against morality, decency, and virtue, private property, socialism, and totalitarianism are more strongly and honestly presented than they are by their own protagonists. Voltaire, the scoffer at Christianity, recognized this. He once boasted that it took twelve men to spread the "infamy" of Christianity, but that it would take only one man to destroy it, and that would be Voltaire himself. In order to arm himself with arguments against Christianity, Voltaire once went to a Benedictine monastery; he lived there for about six months. During this time, news spread about France that Voltaire was about to accept the faith; the truth of the matter is that during these six months Voltaire spent all of his time copying out objections in the writings of Thomas Aquinas, but never reading the answers.

Freud could have found in St. Thomas better arguments for the primacy of the instinct of sex and the psychic life of man than he gives in any of his own writings. St. Thomas actually gives five reasons, and better ones than Freud gives, but he also gives the answers.

Not only does St. Thomas use his reason; not only does he give both sides, but he always maintains that you must argue from the other man's point of view, and not your own. St. Thomas said it was no good to tell an atheist that he is an atheist, nor to berate a man who denies immortality because he equates a man with a beast. He would have said that it makes no sense to attack a Communist on the ground that he is a materialist. His position was that you never can prove a man is wrong on someone else's principles. We must argue with a man on his ground, or not argue with him at all.

Long before pragmatism, Thomas Aquinas was writing on the view that truth is utility, and answering it on the grounds of the pragmatist. Long before Communism, he was arguing against the suppression of private property, but doing so after manifesting a thorough understanding of that position. Long before Freud, he said that doctors "were wont to examine the dreams of the patients in order to determine their psychic state," but without falling into the error of believing that man is to be interpreted in terms of sex.

The great and noble faculty of reason was not given to us to rust unused. Unfortunately, some are even using their reason in order to destroy reason. It is a crazy world when men ask themselves if they have selves, and a mad world when thinkers ask if there is a world. If the modern position that we can never know anything with certainty continues to increase, there is danger that the world may die of skeptic poisoning. It is about time we gave up asking ourselves questions, and began looking for answers. Too long have educators been concerned with extending the frontiers of knowledge and not sufficiently interested in deepening the knowledge that they already possessed. The heart of man was made to be soft; the head of man was meant to be hard. If our brains soften, our hearts will harden. False reason has too long been "the bawd to lust's abuse." May reason, which is the reflection of the light of God in man, be restored to its primacy over feeling, sex, and prejudice. As Sir William Drummond said, "He who will not reason is a bigot; he who cannot is a fool; he who dares not, is a slave."

CHAPTER SIX

Misplaced Infinite

Nothing ever happens in the world that does not first happen in the mind of man. If wrong is rampant in the world, it must be that human minds are wrong, or at least neurotic. Before one can describe the abnormal, we must know what is normal.

The normal mind is represented by this semicircle:

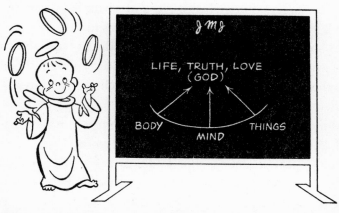

The semicircle is open at the top to indicate the infinity of man's desires, which are basically a desire for Perfect Truth,

Eternal Life, and Ecstatic Love, which is the definition of God.

The normal human being is meant to have open relationships with the eternal or the infinite. Man has a body or flesh, a mind, and a relationship with things in the great world that constitutes his environment.

The normal human being recognizes that his body or his flesh gives him the capacity to experience sensual pleasure or carnal love. This love, as indicated on the drawing, is to be seen as a spark from the great flame of love which is God. Sex love was made not only to deepen affection between husband and wife, not only to be a prolongation of God's creative power to creatures, but also to be a steppingstone to the higher love of God, of which it is the vestibule and the preparation.

The mind of man, when it functions normally, spiritualizes matter. For example, when a piece of chalk is known by the mind, it has a higher existence than it does in the trough of the blackboard. Furthermore, the mind by discovering the truths of science, history, and philosophy, gradually unifies them and sees them as a descent, refraction, and echo of the Great Omniscient Truth, which is God.

Finally, man has a relationship to things outside his body and soul. These things he uses for his comforts, as a material condition for leading a moral life, as a blessing to dispense when superfluous, as a supply for the needs of the poor, and as another reason for thanking God for His Goodness.

To illustrate abnormal living, draw a line across the original design:

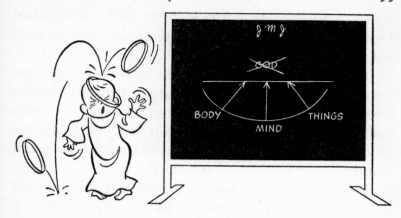

This represents man cutting himself off from God and pro-
claiming his own sufficiency. But man cannot live without a
god; that is impossible. The infinite haunts him constantly. So
he has to make his own gods.

These gods are generally three. The first god is his own
body. Sex pleasure then becomes the supreme goal of life and ultimate happiness. From that point on, he attempts to compensate for a want of eternal divine destiny by the intensity of his
erotic experiences.

Other men make a god of their minds through egotism and
pride and the exaltation of the ego: "There is no knowledge
outside of what I know; there is no law outside of my own
will. I must always be pleased."

The body, made its own limit, becomes sex; the mind, made
its own limit, becomes egotism; the things, denied an extra-
earthly relationship, become the source of greed. Civilization
then becomes a conflict of individual egotisms, each one affirm-

ing his own will—only to have it challenged by his neighbor. From this result jealousies, bickerings, slanders, class conflict, and war.

The third substitute god men make for the true God is the material: wealth, avarice, business, and greed. The true infinite is replaced by the false infinite of "more." Being naked on the inside, such men attempt to cover their nudity by a vain display or aggrandizement of externals, thinking they *are* worth something because they *have* something.

To indicate how man, once he has broken connections with the heavens above, locks himself in his own false temple with his own false god, draw a circle around body, mind, and things, which become misplaced infinities:

Three modern psychiatrists have been concerned with these abnormalities. It is worth noting that psychology today as a science is more concerned with the abnormal than the normal. Freud specializes in sex; Adler, in the inferiority complex; and

Jung, the greatest of all the psychiatrists, is concerned with worldly security. Freud believes man's abnormality is due to the suppression of the *libido*, or sex instinct; the super-ego or morality and convention have given it a false sense of guilt. Adler explains the abnormality by man's desire to escape his deep sense of inferiority, which is basically pride; Jung traces anxieties and neuroses to man's struggle with the basic insecurities of life.

Each is one-third right in discovering the source of abnormalities. If the three ever got together, they would all be right, for then they would be reaffirming that all the unhappiness of man comes from adoration of the three concupiscences: the lust of the flesh, the pride of life, and abnormal love of the world. When sex is uprooted from God, it ceases to be physical-spiritual and becomes psychic and abnormal. When mind denies its creatureliness, it creates within itself a schizoid sensation of superiority; finally, when man loses belief in immortality, he goes mad in an attempt to compensate for it by economic security.

Two effects flow from these misplaced infinities:

1. Anxiety.
2. Despair.

1. *Anxiety*, because man sees a tremendous disproportion between what he *is* and what he *ought* to be. He feels like a fish caught in a net; the more he struggles, the more he becomes entangled. Suffocated in his tiny little world, he is troubled by

always breathing in the same air that he breathes out. He feels like a mountain climber who cannot see the peak of the mountain in the fog, and at the same time trembles lest he tumble into the abyss below. His mind cut off from eternal relationship with God becomes like a reservoir in which the sediment, silt, and scum of life collect. Better could the stem of a rose support a marble bust than the mind of man bear the false infinity of his own deification.

2. *Despair*. Living in a closed circle makes a man despair. He cannot escape the desire for the infinite, and having made himself the infinite, he foresees there is nothing ahead of him but death, annihilation, and destruction. From this comes despair, dread, fear, and trembling. Torn between wanting to be *with* God, and wanting to *be* God, he understands Baudelaire, who said, "The last sacrament of a skeptic is suicide." Disappointed in pleasure, his excesses beget revulsion. Failing to find the infinite within himself, he makes himself the object of dread. He tries to escape self-punishment by anticipating unhappy outcomes, and tries to solace himself with horror movies and vampire stories. He knows he ought to be punished, so he prepares his own punishment.

A modern writer, Franz Kafka, born in Austria in 1893, describes the abnormal, un-Goded man of the twentieth century. Kafka, for example, in his work tells of a surveyor who is bound to report to a superior in a castle, but somehow he never gets to see him. It is always "tomorrow"; maybe "next week." Kafka, under this symbol, presents modern man, who does not quite ever achieve his destiny, simply because life has no moral significance. All is numbness, darkness, and meaninglessness. In another work, *The Trial*, there is Joseph K. No last name, just Joseph K—no tradition, no family background. The courtroom is in total blackness. He does not understand the charge against him, nor why he is condemned; and when he is led out to his death, his last words are "Like a dog."

Kafka is not antimoral, nor anti-God. Kafka was just a modern soul who felt something of the punishment that the Godless soul was experiencing, and was able to describe it well, but could offer no solution. His characters are marionettes, either victims or executioners, because the world is dark and humble and devoid of moral rules.

These and other descriptions do not mean the modern soul is without hope. There are two things that are meant to go together. One is the misery of man: his worries, his trials, his difficulties, his sorrows; the other, the Mercy of God.

Our modern world has split and divorced the two. It has separated the misery of man from the mercy of God. When there is only the misery of man, there is hate, dread, and despair. But as misery without mercy begets despair, so also, as Pascal reminds us, a sense of God's Mercy without a sense of sin and misery can beget presumption, arrogance, and pride. The modern man has already one-half the condition of salvation: he is miserable. The Mercy of God is certainly not wanting. But man must want it, and he wants it when he demands a Redeemer. Then he has peace as he hears, coming from out of the darkness, the plea, "Come to Me, all ye who labor and are heavily burdened, and find rest for your souls."

CHAPTER SEVEN

How to Talk

Many requests have been made to express some ideas on "how to talk." We will treat this subject on two conditions: first, that we be not considered a model speaker or an orator. It is said that I am an orator, and in weak moments I believe it —but only for the reason that when I finish speaking I notice there is always a great "awakening."

A second condition is that any suggestions that we offer are purely personal. Suggestions will be limited to the way we do it and the way we prepare a discourse. Our method is not necessarily the best. A few years ago I was talking in Canada one Sunday afternoon in a theater. Noticing a collection being taken as I spoke, I inquired, "What is the purpose of this collection?" The answer was, "To hire better speakers next year."

The preparation of a discourse. The preparation is both remote and proximate. How long does it take to prepare a speech? How much time is put into a telecast? About thirty or forty years; but this is the remote preparation. It takes only an hour or less to serve dinner to sixty people on an airplane. But the preparation of the dinner actually took months or years. Think of how long it took to grow the carrots, to raise the sheep, to grow potatoes, and to ripen an apple. A good speech, too, has a tremendous remote preparation, and this implies three things: study, study, study. There is no short cut. Delacroix once said, "Rubens is not simple because he has not worked." There is no simple style; there is only style simplified. One has to study science, literature, history, philosophy, forgoing many social evenings just to be alone with one's books. Books are the most wonderful friends in the world. When you meet them and pick them up, they are always ready to give you a few ideas. When you put them down, they never get mad; when you take them up again, they seem to enrich you all the more.

Proximate preparations. Here we will spontaneously let a subject come into the mind to show quickly how it may be given immediate development. Suppose we decide to talk about angels, inasmuch as an angel cleans our blackboard.

First, we would formulate some general ideas, such as:

1. The knowledge of angels.
2. How one angel affects another angel.
3. The function of angels.

Next we would concentrate on some source material to which we would go to find information on angels. The three best sources would be the Scriptures, Thomas Aquinas, and Dionysius. After studying what had been written in these three, we would then fill out our plan.

First, we would show that angels do not know the same

way man knows. We derive all our knowledge from below, *i.e.*, the sensible world, but an angel derives its knowledge from above. Ideas are poured into an angel's mind by God, as we pour water into a glass.

Next, we would consider how angels affect one another; how the superior angels illumine the inferior angels, like water running down a pyramid. Finally, in treating the function of angels we would show how some are before the throne of God, how others preside over creation, while others act as special messengers of God.

After a subject is chosen, say for a telecast, we immediately begin to write out a plan, such as is illustrated above on the subject of angels. We write the general ideas on a sheet of paper; the next day, tear up the paper. The day following we have to start doing it all over again. When that new plan is developed, we tear it up, so that nothing is saved from day to day.

The great advantage of this system is that one is forced to rethink the ideas; the subject is learned from the inside out, instead of from the outside in. Why should the living mind be subject to an inert sheet of paper? A mother does not forget the child of her womb; neither can a mind forget what it has generated by hard thinking.

Today we have only readers on television. There are few speakers any more, and fewer orators. Some believe that what they have written is so sacred that the creative mind ought to bow to a dead message. It is much better, instead of memorizing words, to recreate the ideas each day until the subject is as alive as a child. There may be many mistakes when the time comes to rethink it on your feet, but at least there is this consolation: it is *your* talk. Whenever we hear anyone read a talk, there is always the temptation to ask, "Who wrote it?"

Much wisdom is hidden in the remark of the old Irishwoman who heard a Bishop reading his discourse. She said, "Glory be to God, if he can't remember it, how does he expect us to?"

Three conditions of **a good talk** are sincerity, clarity, and flexibility.

Sincerity. To have sincerity is to be without affectation, pose, or cultivated airs; just being oneself. The word "sincere" has an interesting origin. When the Romans found pieces of marble that were imperfect, they put wax in the holes. Wax, in Latin, is *cera*. When they found a perfect piece of marble, it was called *sine cera*, or without wax, whence comes the word "sincere." A sincere speaker is one without guile or artfulness. If the tongue gives forth an uncertain sound, who will prepare for battle?

One of the first rules in speaking is: Do not imitate Bishop Sheen. No imitator is sincere. Be yourself! Every person is unique and incommunicable. There is something about him that is worth more than the material universe. Having his own tempo, his own spirit, his own disposition, he ought to speak out of that, and he will be interesting.

Insincerity often is derived from a want of conviction or truthfulness. So many people say things they do not mean that when they really want to drive home a conviction they lack the power to move. How different is the tone of the voice of an announcer when he reads his commercial, and when he describes a Baseball game. He does not believe in the commercial, so he lacks sincerity. Lincoln once said that he liked to hear a man talk as if he were fighting bees. Too often men dedicated to religion pray in public, either as if they were giving marching orders to God, or as if they were more interested in the audience than in God. In some instances, it would be better to tell the audience to pray, rather than to pray *to* them.

A lesson in sincerity was given me in college. I was chosen for the debating team; the night before the Notre Dame debate, our professor of debating called me to his office and scolded me: "You are absolutely rotten. We have never had anybody in the history of this college who was a worse speaker than yourself." "Well," I said, trying to justify myself, "if I am so rotten, why did you pick me for the team?" "Because," he answered, "you can think; not because you can talk. Get over in that corner. Take a paragraph of your speech and go through it." I repeated it over and over again for an hour, at the end of which he said, "Do you see any mistake in that?" "No." Again, an hour and a half, two hours, two and a half hours, at the end of which I was exhausted. He said, "Do you still not see what is wrong?" Being naturally quick, after two hours and a half, I caught on. I said, "Yes. I am not sincere. I am not my-self. I do not talk as if I meant it." His final injunction was, "Now you are ready to speak."

As Shakespeare expressed it:

> . . . to thine own self be true,
> And it must follow as the night the day,
> Thou canst not then be false to any man.

Clarity. Clarity is derived from understanding a subject. A professor in a class in cosmology once asked me the definition of time. I said, "I know what it is, but I can't tell you." He said, "If you knew what it is, you could tell me."

The reason why professors are dull in class is because they do not understand their subject. The ordinary teacher of physics could not tell an uneducated person anything about the mathematics of space-time. But Eddington and Jeans have done so, because they knew the subject profoundly. It is easy to write a book with footnotes, because everything you do not understand or do not grasp thoroughly you put down at the bottom of the page, so that someone else can look it up. But to write on that same subject so that children in the seventh or eighth grade can understand it, one must really understand the subject.

The ideal talk possesses clarity for both the educated and the simple when it combines the abstract principles or scientific description with concrete examples or analogies. The educated can follow both; the uneducated can grasp the idea at least vaguely through illustrations drawn from their own experience. Our Blessed Lord, Who is the Eternal Word, did not disdain to use parables to make mysteries clearer to our finite minds. One must always know more about a subject than one gives in a speech. As the lungs must have the atmosphere, as the eye must have more light than that which enters it, so the mind, to breathe easily on a subject, must have a great environment of knowledge.

Clarity is aided by telling the audience what you are going to do. Give them the points of the discourse. Then they know at least when you are going to finish. Otherwise, if one appears with a sheaf of papers, the audience after an hour may sigh, "He has got two inches more to go." At a philosophical convention, a speaker was reading a paper on "Essence and Existence" for an hour and a half. The listeners were exhausted until he looked up from his paper and said, "I forgot to tell you. I have three carbon copies here of my speech." It was such a relief!

In television, one must always time himself from the end, not the beginning. Decide how many minutes one needs for the conclusion. Suppose it is three minutes. Then just three minutes before the appointed time, swinging gracefully from the body of the talk to the conclusion, one finishes "right on the nose."

· *Flexibility*. Readers should always be prepared to skip over about eighty-nine pages if they see the audience is tiring. Then, too, there may be interruptions; someone faints, or one may be heckled. A speaker was once addressing a group of lawyers. One lawyer was in a terrible state of "amiable incandescence." He stood up, shouting something which nobody understood. As everyone turned to him, the speaker said, "You have been practicing at the wrong bar."

I recall a drunk once standing up in the gallery, heckling in a most unintelligible manner. After failing to catch his words, I seemed to satisfy him with the observation, "The only man that likes to be interrupted in the middle of a sentence is a prisoner."

Once, while I was giving instructions to a convert class in Washington on the Blessed Trinity, someone began to heckle me about Jonas: "How was Jonas in the belly of the whale for three days?" I said, "My good man, I do not know. But," I said, "when I get to heaven I will ask Jonas." He said, "Suppose Jonas is not there?" I said, "Then you ask him."

On another occasion, while I was preaching in a small country parish, a mother, embarrassed by her crying infant, left the pew to leave the church. I said, "Madam, it is quite all right. The child isn't bothering me." She said, "I know, but you are bothering the child."

Flexibility is increased when one does not have the speech

memorized; then one can make use of any occasion that may arise in the course of the discourse. Recall the beautiful impromptu speeches of Our Blessed Lord such as the one to the woman at the well, when He turned the subject of thirst into the idea of the soul's yearning for God.

More important than the above factors in preparing a discourse is to recognize that every speaker is the trustee of God's truth. When we speak, we are only the flute; it is God who breathes on us. We supply only the quality of tone—nothing else.

Prayer and meditation are essentials for a truthful message. The last thing I do before giving a talk is to go into the chapel, kneel down before Our Lord and the Blessed Sacrament, and say to Him, "Give me strength, tonight, to speak Thy Truth, that Thou mayest be known, not me; the power to make others love Thee, but not that I may be loved. Instill in those who listen to me a love of Thee, so that there may not be only truth communicated, but also a love of that truth."

Light and heat are inseparable in fire, and they ought to be inseparable in anyone who gives a discourse. The light is God's truth; the heat is the tremendous love with which one ought to communicate the truth. To love what we say, it must be true. To want to speak the truth, it must be loved.

CHAPTER EIGHT

Inferiority Complex

The "inferiority complex," as an expression and as a scientific idea, was given to the world by the psychologist Alfred Adler. If adequate means could be found for asserting superiority, no one would suffer, it is said, from an inferiority complex. But though everyone is anxious to achieve superiority, few ever actually attain it. When a person does not achieve it, he sometimes will compensate for it by a substitute behavior, in which there is hidden a drive for superiority; the indirect way of asserting this superiority produces an "inferiority complex."

There are several kinds of inferiority complexes, for example, physical. When a woman is too fat, this makes her feel very inferior in the company of thin women. A fat woman went to a gymnasium. The instructor said she would have to chin herself twenty times a day. She asked, "Which chin?"

There is also social inferiority, for example, the little girl who said, "Grandma, why do I always have to wear overalls? The other girls can wear overalls only for fun." There is the economic inferiority due to having a Chevrolet in a Buick neighborhood or else having been born on the other side of the tracks.

How the inferiority complex works can be explained by a parable of a muskrat coat that suffered from an inferiority complex because he wanted to be a mink coat.

The muskrat coat wore a very expensive silk lining on the inside of which initials were embroidered. The muskrat coat always wore his sleeves rolled back, because they looked more like an expensive mink that way. The muskrat coat always wore a price tag on the back: "$7,500—genuine ranch mink." He always liked to parade on Fifth Avenue in company with minks; when the summer came, he always went into cold storage with mink coats. He never would go to a cheap storage, where there were cheap muskrat coats like himself.

But the poor muskrat had his difficulties. Despite the fact

that he wore "mink perfume" all the time, he knew that minks were rather hardy and that you could sit on a mink. He loved to be sat on, to prove he was a mink. But he couldn't take it. It told "in the end." He stayed away from the movies, because he was afraid of sitting next to a muskrat coat who might recognize him. He would never have felt this inferiority, if he had not been trying to be what he was not. So he went to a psychiatrist, who put the muskrat on the couch and began asking all kinds of questions.

The psychiatrist after a while explained, "You know the trouble with you? Your mother was frightened by a mink." The psychiatrist finally told the poor muskrat coat that he would have to be given a shock treatment. The shock treatment consisted in the muskrat being put into a cabinet with minks. When the minks heard of it, they said one to another, "I smell a rat."

They got so angry, they pulled the hair out of the muskrat. The shock treatments did not help him one bit. From then on, he walked the streets of New York saying he was the only bald mink in New York. He had an incurable inferiority complex!

Human beings, in a modern age which knows no humility, strive for a false superiority, either directly or indirectly; *i.e.*, they play it straight, or they play it crooked. They who have an undue sense of superiority and play it straight become the Malenkovs of the dictator type. They are overbearing, loud, critical, and proud, and constantly use the pronoun "I." Vain people like to prove themselves right, especially in argument. What is important is not the *truth* of things, but their being *right*.

The Soviets know that industrially they cannot keep abreast of the United States. The Soviets cover up this sense of inferiority by claiming to be the inventors of every modern convenience. When Soviet diplomats leave America to return to their slave state, they load themselves with radios and refrigerators and electric typewriters. How else could they "invent" these things unless they brought them back? The Soviets know they have enslaved millions of people. In the face of the freedom and humanism of the Western world they have a sense of inferiority. To overcome it, they accuse the Western world of being a slave civilization. This gives them for the moment a feeling of superiority.

Other forms of the direct quest for superiority are to be found in "loud mouths" who seek to attract attention by noise, or who give the impression of being good fellows by shaking hands with you all the way to the elbow. Others wear loud shirts, so suspicious are they that others may not notice their superiority. Still others wear loud socks—so loud that their feet never go to sleep. Just as there are women who dress badly deliberately, because if they dressed well they would be exposed to ridicule, so there are professors who never write a book, because they are afraid of being criticized.

Indirect quests for superiority manifest themselves in the dreamers. Unable to achieve superiority in real life, they live in a world of fantasy in which they believe themselves superior. A boy who gets sick just before examination time may see that he cannot realize his fantasy, so he develops a nervous breakdown. Without pain, he would have been forced to prove the greatness or the smartness of which he boasted. Failure to pass would have meant giving up the pretense. The bubble of fantasy would have been pricked. Dressing in rags in a studied and calculated manner may be one's way of getting credit for being a friend of the proletariat.

Ever notice how many university libraries in the United States have been given by men who hardly ever went beyond the seventh or eighth grade? This may be due in a few instances, to their conscious inferiority in the field of culture and education; so they endow libraries. "See how educated I am?"

A very well-known man made a fortune after he invented dynamite. He constructed plants to build dynamite throughout the world; then he realized all the harm, actual and possible, that comes with war. His sense of inferiority may have explained leaving an endowment for peace, called after him, the Nobel peace prize.

The worm-eaters are different from the dreamers. They cover up their desire for superiority by minimizing themselves. They are so "humble." "Nobody loves me." They are always threatening to go out in the garden to eat worms. They love exile to the doghouse, and are proud of it! "Pay no attention to me. Nobody cares." Students who belittle their work to get praise from professors are worm-eaters. Communists are worm-eaters. They love to be put in jail, so everyone will say, "See? He is a hero."

Another class of egotists are the "talebearing" animals; by this is meant those who have a fine sense of rumor. They give anybody the benefit of the dirt. They are never happy unless they can get something on somebody. Then they whisper it around and thus try to make themselves superior to others by pointing out the vices and the inferiority of others.

Sometimes those who most inordinately accuse others of a certain fault have a strong inclination to that same fault. Our Divine Lord said, "Judge not and ye will not be judged." Here it is suggested that our judgment of others is a projection of our own weakness. How can one woman call another "catty" unless she has some experience of "cattiness"? Politicians call one another "crooked"—an accusation which is not always born of a love of honesty.

These examples of the inferiority complex reveal that it is really a *superiority complex*. It is not anything new. We have always known it as pride. Pride is an undue estimation and an inordinate esteem of one's own excellence. Most people really do not suffer from a sense of inferiority, but a sense of superiority. Pride is an insoluble particle that resists fusion and protests against amalgamation. Externals are made substitutes for the internal. Excessive luxury in dress often indicates an inner nudity. The ego is a shell incasing the real self. The more entrenched we become in our pride, the harder becomes this shell.

Pride is at its peak when man cuts himself off from any relation to God and thus makes himself god. He elevates his relative character into an absolute, very much like a carbon copy calling itself the original. The pendulum of a clock is free to swing so long as it is attached to the mechanism; but once it becomes detached, it is no longer free to swing. Man is free when he has a point of suspension to God. When he alienates himself in a false independence, he eventually grows tired of his false freedom. Eventually he looks around for someone to whom he can give up his freedom, which begins to bore him. Dictators supply that function in modern civilization. As individuals surrender their responsibility, they create socialism in its tyrannical form. The false superiority some give themselves is a kind of anesthesia to deaden the pain of being plain fools.

The cure for it is to be found in the revival of that forgotten virtue of humility. Humility does not mean a submissiveness, a passiveness, a willingness to be walked on, or a desire to live in the doghouse. Humility is a virtue by which we recognize ourselves as we really are, not as we would like to be in the eyes of the public; not as our press notices say we are, but as we are in the sight of God when we examine our conscience.

Egotism is a failing for which we have to compensate. Poverty is a peril and a disgrace only to those who want to be rich. Obscurity is a menace only to those who want the plaudits of men.

Humility always is thankful for a talent, but conscious of

its limitations. For example, a wood carver has the capacity to make statues, but if he is humble, he will never develop a complex trying to cover up the fact that he is not a watch-maker. A scientist will be proud of his talent of being able to read the universe in terms of mathematics, and he will thank God for the gift. But if he is a humble man, he will recognize his limitations, and not write a book on "The Idea of God" —unless he also possesses the talent of a philosopher.

There would be no humility if, after appearing week after week on television, one said, "Oh, I cannot talk. I do not know how to express an idea. I have no words to explain anything. There are a hundred million other people in the United States who could do this better than I can." Such a speaker should thank the Good Lord for blessing him with the talent, for giving him an education, for giving him an opportunity to speak the truth.

But such a speaker should recognize his limitations and not attempt to dance a ballet or sing an opera. A six-foot-tall man is not humble if he says he is only four feet tall, nor is he humble if he says he is taller than any other man who ever lived. It is only when we recognize our inferiority that we become superior to others. "He that humbleth himself shall be exalted." Those who most suppress their own egos are always the most popular.

In relation to our neighbor, we will recognize that if he had our talents and our opportunities and our graces, he would have done much more with them. The humble person will always look for what is worst in himself, but what is best in his neighbor. His rule will be that of John the Baptist: "He must increase; I must decrease." As soon as we begin to see our own limitations, we perceive perfection in others. Heaven is very high, but the gate to it is very low. To enter we must stoop; bending the ego is the condition of entering therein, and that requires the virtue of humility.

CHAPTER NINE

Fatima

Our modern world with its great crises began on October 13, 1917. Three cities will quickly be visited to see what happened on that day: Moscow, Rome, and a little village in Portugal called Fatima.

October 13, 1917—Moscow. Maria Alexandrovich, a young Russian noblewoman, was teaching religion to a class of two hundred children in the Church of the Iberian Virgin. Suddenly there was a disturbance; horsemen entered the front door, rode madly down the middle aisle, vaulted the communion rail, destroyed the icons, the statuary, and the altar, then turned on the children, killing many of them.

Maria Alexandrovich ran out of the church screaming. Knowing there was an imminent revolution and suspecting the leader of them all, she went to him, saying, "A most terrible thing has happened. I was teaching catechism to my children when horsemen came in, charged them, and killed some of them." The revolutionist leader said, "I know it. I sent them." Such was one of the events that heralded the beginning of the terrible Communist Revolution that has since harassed the world.

Rome—October 13, 1917—the same hour of midday. Church bells are ringing throughout the city, heralding a joyful event: the consecration of a bishop. His name—Eugenio Pacelli—a man who then was not very well known, but who one day would become the greatest spiritual force in the world against the revolutionary tyranny of Communism.

After his consecration on that thirteenth day of October, 1917, he went to Munich. At that particular time the Communists had started a revolution on April 7, 1917, under the leadership of a sailor, Rudolph Egelhofer, and two Bolshevik Commissars, Levine and Axelrod, who set up a Soviet republic. Calling themselves Spartacists, and rising under the leadership of Karl Liebknecht and Rosa Luxemburg, Communist gunmen roamed the streets. A Red army was created, which, going into action, killed 325 people on April 25 in Munich alone. They had raked with machine-gun fire the home of the man who, unmoved by threats, had mounted the pulpit of the Munich cathedral against the orders of the Red committee. Finally, they decided to assassinate him. On April 29 at three o'clock in the afternoon, Commander Seiler of the Red Army of the South and his aide-de-camp Brongratz, armed with orders from Egelhofer, appeared at the door of his house in company with a group of Red sailors. The thugs, gaining entrance to the house by threatening the servant with hand grenades, made their way to the library and with guns drawn awaited the appearance of their prey. Seiler took up his appearance closest to the door with a pistol drawn; the soldiers stood around in a semicircle, some with drawn guns, some with hand grenades.

Suddenly the wanted man appeared. With a blasphemy, Seiler threw out his pistol hand and as he did it hit the pectoral cross on the man's breast. This tall lean figure, grasping the pectoral cross and facing the raised guns, said in soft, low tones. "All right—kill me! But you gain nothing! I am only trying to save Germany."

Under the gaze of those spiritual eyes no one dared pull a trigger. Neither Seiler nor Brongratz nor the soldiers knew why they did not shoot; when they got back to headquarters, they were unable to explain to Egelhofer why they did not kill that man. They were never able to explain why a pair of eyes, a lean figure holding a cross, and a soft voice should be more powerful than their guns, grenades, and orders. There was only one thing that was certain. From that day on that man was afraid of absolutely nothing in all the world. And his name? Eugenio Pacelli, the future Pope Pius XII.

That pectoral cross which he was wearing that night, I am wearing now. Pius XII gave it to his esteemed friend, His Eminence, Cardinal Spellman, who loaned it to me for this telecast.

October 13, 1917. Near the little village of Fatima three little children, Lucy, Jacinta, and Francis, were gathered, expecting a revelation. They had said that Mary, the Mother of God, had appeared to them. It would not be surprising if she had, not only because the Lord came through her, not only because through her He worked His first miracle, and not only because from the Cross He commended us to her with His kind words, "Behold thy mother," but above all, because being the Mother of mankind she should have a motherly interest in our troubles during the twentieth century.

The children said the Lady had appeared to them before, on April 13, May 13, June 13, and July 13, August 19, and September 13. In the course of these earlier revelations, something very interesting was said which goes to show that our world conditions are determined by the way we live rather than by politics.

The Lady said that the present World War, which was World War I, would end in a little over another year. The United States went to war on Good Friday of that year, 1917. Actually, the war did end in a little over another year, on November 11, 1918.

The Lady told the children that there would come an era of peace to the world *if* the world would only return to God; Russia in that case would be converted. But she added, "If people do not stop offending God, another and worse World War will have its remote beginning during the reign of the next Pontiff." This, it was disclosed, was the Civil War in Spain. World War II could have been prevented by penance and prayer and return again to God. For the failure of the world to return to God, the Virgin foretold another World War: "Russia will spread her errors throughout the world, promoting wars and persecutions. The good will be martyred, the Holy Father will have to suffer much, and various nations will be annihilated."

The Blessed Virgin promised the children that on October 13, 1917, she would give a sign that her revelation was true. Seventy thousand people gathered at Fatima on that rainy day with the children, awaiting a sign. Most of them were unbelievers. Portugal in those days was an anarchistic, Communistic, anticlerical, and atheistic nation. Most of the people came out of curiosity, not out of faith. They doubted that anything would happen, but the children assured them that the Heavenly Lady would show a great sign as a proof that she had actually appeared. The proof was what has since been called the "Miracle of the Sun." The testimony of these 70,000 people, as well as the records of the atheistic and anarchistic newspapers of the time which I have read, attested the fact of what happened. One anarchistic newspaper stated that there was a miracle of the sun, but it hoped that nobody would interpret it in a Divine way.

The Blessed Mother first appeared to the children and then pointed to the sun as a rift in the clouds made it visible. The sun seemed almost to detach itself from the heavens, becoming like a great silver ball; shooting sparks in all directions, it seemed to descend to the earth as if about to precipitate itself upon the people. Immediately they all cried out to God in prayer and supplication, in sorrow and in contrition. Three times the sun became a whirling mass of flashing silver and, spinning on its axis, cast off beams of multicolored light, as it plunged and zigzagged its way to the earth. The crowd shrank in fear and clamored for mercy as the molten mass seemed about to destroy them. And though it rained all day, after the miracle of the sun had taken place three times, everyone discovered that their clothes were dry.

From that time on, Fatima became a kind of gathering place of all the people of the world who believed that peace is made somewhere else than at the tables of the politicians. The Heavenly Lady had told them that peace was conditioned on prayer, expiation, and sacrifice. On October 13, 1951, I was at Fatima when a million people gathered there to pray for peace. They had gathered the night before during one of those cold rains so common to Portuguese mountaintops; all through that wet night, they either stood or knelt as they prayed for the peace of the world. I stayed with them until three o'clock, when I was offered a cot. But I could not sleep. The luxury of a cot is unbearable when there are a million people staying up all night in prayer to beg peace for a war-weary world. The only thing to do was to get out of bed and pray with them through the night for the peace of the world.

The next morning as the statue of Our Lady of Fatima was carried through the throng, these million people waved white handkerchiefs as white flags of purity, in tribute to the Lady of Peace. One's mind suddenly left that White Square of Fatima and went to the Red Square of Moscow, where there were flags, dyed red in the blood of the victims. Somehow one felt that the White Square was giving the only answer there is to the Red Square. A great change seemed to come over the Communist hammer and the sickle. The hammer that had beaten down so many homes, and profaned so many sanctuaries, will one day, in virtue of such prayer and penance, be held aloft by millions of men and begin to look like a cross; the sickle which the Communists used to cut human life like unripe wheat will also change its symbolism and begin to look as "the moon under the Lady's feet."

World War II would not have happened if men had returned to God. World War III need not happen, and it will not happen if we as a nation return to God. If there is a cold war in the world, it is because our hearts and our souls are not on fire with the love of God.

It may be worth inquiring, however, why Almighty God in His providential dealings with the universe should see fit in this day to give us a revelation of His Blessed Mother in order to bring us back to prayer and penance.

One reason immediately comes to mind. Since the world has lost Christ, it may be that through Mary it will recover Him. When Our Blessed Lord was lost at the age of twelve, it was the Blessed Mother who found Him. Now that He has been lost again, it may be through Mary that the world will recover Christ their Saviour. Another reason is that Divine Providence has committed to a woman the power of overcoming evil. In that first dread day when evil was introduced into the world, God spoke to the serpent in the Garden of Eden and said, "I shall put enmity between thee and the woman; between thy seed and her seed, and thou shalt lie in wait for her heel" (Gen. 3:15). In other words, evil shall have a progeny and a seed. Goodness, too, shall have a progeny and a seed. It will be through the power of the woman that evil will be overcome. We live now in an evil hour, for though goodness has its day, evil does have its hour. Our Blessed Lord said that much the night that Judas came into the garden: "This is your hour, the power of darkness" (Luke 22:53). All evil can do in that hour is to put out the lights of the world; but it can do that. If then we live in an evil hour, how shall we overcome the spirit of Satan except by the power of that Woman to whom Almighty God has given the mandate to crush the head of the serpent?

CHAPTER TEN

Content with Sawdust Brains?

If one came into a city a perfect stranger and saw people hilarious, gay, and happy, exchanging gifts and greetings with one another, and abounding in good cheer, but with no apparent reason for such happiness, one would wonder if they were out of their heads.

Once a year, at Christmas time, everyone is happy and loving, kind and generous. But one wonders if they know why they are happy. The reason for the joy and happiness of Christmas we will explain with dolls—but before doing so, a word about what Christmas has done to Time, Space, and the Missing Link.

Christmas did something to Time. Everyone is born in a certain era of time over which he has no control. But when Eternity came to this earth and established His beachhead in Bethlehem, Time was struck with such a terrific impact that it was split in two. From that moment on, all the periods of history have been divided into the period before Christ (B.C.) and the period after Christ (A.D.), *Anno Domini*, the year of the Lord. Even the Communists, who deny God, nevertheless date all of their newspapers as so many years after His birth.

Not only was Time split in two, but Space was turned upside down. The Greeks believed that their Gods dwelt on Olympian heights. This worried them to some extent, because if God is "way up there," what does He know about our sufferings? They wanted a God Who was in the dust of human lives. What did a God in the heights know about being a refugee, about being homeless? Was He ever betrayed? Did He ever suffer? Did He ever come close to death? But when the Son of God was born under the floor of the world in Bethlehem, He shook the world to its very foundations. More than that, He turned Space upside down. Until then, mothers always used to say, as they held children in their arms, "Heaven is way, way up there"; but the day that the Woman held the Babe in her arms, it began to be true to say that she "looked down" to Heaven.

Finally, Christmas is the discovery of the Missing Link. During the last one hundred years scholars have been concerned about finding man's relationship to the beast. Distressingly enough during that same period of time, man has almost acted like a beast. Christmas is the discovery of the Missing Link—not the link that binds man to the beast, but the link that binds man to God. The Divine Babe was the real Cave Man, for He was born in a cave of Bethlehem. The light that is shining in His eyes is not that of a beast coming to the dawn of reason, but the light of God coming to the darkness of men; His name is not Piltdown, but Christ. Being God and Man, He is the link between both. Life is now discovered to be not a push from below, but a gift from above.

Now we come to the explanation of Christmas. Remember the song the doll sang after having been repaired, and how she wondered if the little girl would love her after she got back from the doll hospital?

I'm a little doll who was dropped and broken
Falling off my mommy's knees;
I'm a little doll who has just been mended;
Now, won't you tell me please
Are my ears on straight?
Is my nose in place?
Have I got a cute expression on my face?
Are my blue eyes bright?
Do I look all right to be taken home Christmas day?

When I first came here just a month ago
Brought in by a little girl who loved me so,
She began to cry 'til they told her
I could be taken home Christmas day.

Christmas time is drawing nearer and I'm getting scared;
Wish I could see in a mirror how I've been repaired.
I'll be called for soon but I've worried so;
Will she love me like she did a month ago?
Are my ears on straight?
I can hardly wait to be taken home Christmas day.

Christmas is the repairing of human nature or human dolls. Here are a number of broken dolls.

Which one of these two has the Toni? This one has an Italian haircut—it looks like spaghetti. This one has a hole in his head; he is very open-minded. This one was asked whether or not he was a loyal American: he hid behind the Fifth Amendment and lost his head to Russia. And this is the only one in the lot who asked for a woman's hand, and he found for the rest of his life that he was under her thumb.

Picture a little girl called Gundy standing before these broken dolls, asking them, not if they would like to be repaired, but if they would like to become live dolls, or little girls and boys. She says, "You have only sawdust brains, and you have a rag heart; you have no life in you. Wouldn't you like to be alive just as I am?" She told the dolls that if they willed to become alive, they would know things they did not know now; that they would begin to love and make sacrifices for one another; that a new and higher form of energy would flow through their bodies and minds. But she failed to convince

the dolls. Some went off to a psychoanalyst to have their sawdust examined. Among the others, one sneered, saying, "How
do we know there is any such thing as the life beyond ours?
We know only sawdust." Another doll asks, "That means we
have to get cleaned up, doesn't it, and we like to be dirty."

The little girl wondered what she could do to induce the
dolls to become little girls. She recalled a lady who could make
the most beautiful doll that ever lived, though she never made
a doll. Gundy sent an angel to this beautiful lady and asked
her to make a live doll that would be so lovely that all the poor
little rag dolls would want to be like her.

These dolls represent human nature—battered and weary,
worn, full of anxieties and fears; they have a knowledge, but
it is incomplete; aspirations for goodness, but lacking power
to implement that desire; then, too, there is in them a kind of
drag toward evil.

As the little girl asked the dolls to become alive, so God
asked mankind to become not just creatures but His children,
so that His Life would vibrate in their souls. God could have
forced faith on man's mind and a higher love on his will, but
He did not want to destroy human freedom. He sent an angel
to the most beautiful woman who ever lived, asking her, "Will
you give Me a human nature, so that I Who am God, may become man?" The woman answered, "Fiat"—"Be it done."
God's purpose was to show man all that He was destined to
be from the beginning. The Woman was to give Him a human
nature like ours in all things save sin. I have a body; I have
a soul; the nature of each is different, despite the need of one

for the other; but I am still one person. So in the God-man, or Christ, in a perfect manner was united the nature of man and the nature of God, in the unity of the Person of God.

As Gundy wanted to make rag dolls live dolls, God wanted to change our nature, so that we would *become* something we are not, through the Power He would give us. After all, did not lower creation reveal that, thanks to something above them, chemicals were being transformed into plants, plants into animals, and all three into man? Why should not man be transformed into something Divine? Not that man would ever be as Divine as God is, but man could in some way share His nature, and thus have added to his human reason the light of faith.

Through our own fault we had lost resemblance to the God Who made us. By being born of our parents we are not sons of God; God is not our Father unless we share His Life. The oxygen does not live in the plant unless the plant takes it up unto itself; far less could we share the Divine Life unless He came from Heaven to give it to us. It is not nearly as big a change for a stone to become a fish, as it is for a man to become a child of God.

When He came to this earth, it was not to give us a code; it was not to give us a law; it was not to have some secretaries write books that we might read as we read Plato or Socrates. It was rather that we might be endowed with His Divine Life, and be not just men, but heirs of Heaven and sons of the Eternal Father.

On Christmas Day, this process began for men of good will. Eternity came to Time and housed Himself in the flesh ciborium of His Blessed Mother. The Mother and Babe cannot be separated. Those who attempt to do so soon separate Christ from Christmas. His Mother, being of royal blood, obeyed an order of Caesar Augustus to be enrolled in the ancestral village of Bethlehem. "There was no room in the inn" for the God Who made the earth. One cannot help asking today if there is room in the U.N.? Out to a shepherd's cave went the Mother; there in a manger where beasts eat, He Who called Himself the "Living Bread descended from Heaven" is born in Bethlehem, the "House of Bread." In all other religions, man toils to get to God; in Christianity, God first comes to man, and *then* man goes to God.

Omnipotence is in bonds; Eternity in Time. The bird that built the nest of earth is hatched therein. He Who is born without a Mother in heaven, is born without a father on Earth. He Who made His Mother, is born of His Mother. Maker of the sun is under the sun; Molder of the earth is on the earth; Ineffable Wisdom, a little infant, filling the world, lying in a manger; ruling the universe, suckling a breast. Liberty becomes captive, the Master a servant; the Eternal Word is Dumb! This is the mystery of Christmas: God becoming a man that man might become God-like.

Each succeeding Christmas confronts each soul with the query, "What does it profit Christ to be born in Bethlehem a thousand times, unless He is also born in our own hearts?" Not everyone wants to be born to Him; many are like the little dolls. Not every doll wanted to be cleaned. Some doubted there was a life higher and beyond sawdust existence. But those who did want their nature changed found themselves living in a different world with a cleaner mind and a deeper love, and they are so very, very happy. What a pity so many go through life with sawdust brains, rag hearts, and loveless bodies!

Christmas is not something that has happened; it is something that is happening. The real problem is something like that of the doll, though we change the words to read, "Is my heart on straight? Is my soul in place? Do I have a love expression on my face? Is my soul full of God's light? Do I look all right to be taken to the crib on Christmas morn?"

CHAPTER ELEVEN

Altruism: The Evolution of Love

Our world has been too much impressed by both Darwin and Marx; it is not correct to believe that life is to be explained in terms of the Darwinian struggle for existence and the Marxist terms of class conflict. Tennyson was not wholly right in describing "nature red in tooth and claw," for the truth is that most teeth and claws are not red but green with chlorophyll and life.

A more scientific view of nature sees it, not only as a scene of struggle, but also as a stage for altruism. Nature is full of cooperation, affection, harmony, benevolence, chivalry, generosity, in which the chord of self is struck in order to make music for others. Take a survey of nature and it will be discovered that it is unconsciously preparing for love in man.

Consider first the sun. It is over 92 million miles away from this earth, yet it is burning itself away at the rate of 365,000 tons a day in order to light this world. Sunbeams are shining ghosts of defunct matter; electrons and protons are falling into each other's arms and vanishing into radiation for the sake of the earth.

Volcanoes, in their turn, after the crashing of suns and planets, are less bent on the destruction of life than on being a nursery for it. The water that is on the earth was formed from the condensed steam of primitive volcanoes. Minerals dissolved from these hot streams as they hissed from the crater's mouth and drooling lips. Rolling down the sides of the volcanoes, they became streams and rivers and oceans. The chemicals in these waters prepared for blood. Nature did not draw blood from stone, but from red-hot lava. In a certain sense, the volcanoes suffered a veritable hemorrhage of blood, for the primitive sea contained all of the mineral salts, albuminous substances, and oxygen which the first sea creatures needed. Mammalian blood has ingeniously maintained the original temperature of 99 to 100°F., and is still a solution of 8 parts in 1,000 of some twenty or more chemical salts. The Greeks used to say that all life came from water. Maybe they were not so wrong, for Our Blessed Lord certainly said that Divine Life came from water: "Unless a man be born again of water and the Holy Ghost."

Plants, too, tell us not only that life must live for itself, but also for others. The trunk and the branches are for self, but the blossoms are for a generation yet unborn. The lesson of altruism is hidden in every blossom. The blossom is one of the first blushes of motherhood that nature knows. So much is the noble tree bound up with altruism that ofttimes reproduction is hastened by wounding it, as if to remind us that sacrifice and surrender is the condition of a new and richer life. When an apple falls to the ground, the outer pulp decays and rots, but inside of it are seeds which are the promise of immortality. This may be a dim suggestion that when we shuffle off our mortal coil, there is hidden within the outer pulp, a soul which is the seed of true immortality.

In pre-Bolshevik days, a distinguished Russian scientist by the name of Timiriazeff planted a willow tree weighing 5 pounds in 200 pounds of soil. After 5 years he took out the tree, weighed it, and found that it had increased to 169 pounds 3 ounces. Carefully weighing the soil, he discovered that there had been a loss of only 2 ounces. The increase of over 164 pounds in the weight of the willow was due to its nourishment and communion with the great, invisible forces of light and heat. Lower nature is not the sole explanation of growth of the tree. This is a dim reminder that man's true growth is through communion with the spiritual forces which issue from the Heart of God.

One of the lowest forms of animal life is the amoeba; while it has to struggle for its own existence, it also suggests thoughtfulness for others. The amoeba has only one cell; yet there comes a moment in its life when it has to decide whether or not it will live only for itself, or sacrifice a part of itself in order that another life may live. As it reproduces itself by fission, or splitting, there is a physical forecast of something noble in the universe. Unconsciously it perceives that it must either reproduce itself or die; it saves the species by sacrifice, and thus is a kind of Old Testament preparation for the higher love in man. All through nature, those communities which include the greatest number of sympathetic members flourish best; those which manifest the greatest mutual aid have the best chance of survival. Nature is never purposefully cruel.

Love begins to be conscious in man. In nature, altruism is necessary; in man, it is free. It is the possibility of "no" which gives so much charm to "yes."

There are five ways in which man can love his fellow man. The first is *utilitarian* love, which is directed to another because he is useful to us. "He can get it at wholesale." "He knows where to buy minks at a discount." The difficulty with this kind of love is that when the advantage is lost, the friendship no longer endures.

The second kind of love is *romantic*, or sex, love. This is the kind of affection we bear to another because of the pleasure which the other person gives us. The "I" is projected into the "thou," and though the thou is pretended to be loved, actually what is loved is the "I" that is in it. One of the reasons why many modern marriages do not endure is because people do not marry a person: they marry an experience. They fall in love with an ecstasy or a thrill, loving the cake only as long as it has frosting on it.

The third kind of love that one can have for another is *democratic* love, which is based upon equality under the law. Others are respected because they are fellow citizens; or their liberties are recognized, in order that ours, in their turn, may be recognized. The reason for contributing to the good of others is the expectation of a return good. Democratic love, however, functions only up to a certain point; it is often subtracted in competition, or else invalidated on the assumption that the other person is "not worthy" of our affection. Democratic love is often under a great strain during a political campaign as candidates call one another "cheap politicians." There is no such thing in all the world as a "*cheap* politician."

The fourth kind of love, which has given much inspiration to poetry, is *humanitarian* love, which is love for humanity in general. One of the defects of this type of love is that it is love in the abstract, rather than in the concrete; it is love at a distance, rather than an immediate service. It is a historical fact that those who have most proclaimed their love of humanity have found it very difficult to love certain human beings. Humanity is like a composite photograph: it is nobody in particular. Dostoievski makes one of his better characters describe the insufficiency of this type of love: "I love humanity but I wonder at myself, because the more I love humanity in general, the less I love man in particular. In my dreams I have come to make enthusiastic schemes for the service of humanity, and perhaps I might actually have faced a crucifixion had it been suddenly necessary, and yet, I am incapable of living in the same room with anyone two days together, as I know by experience. As soon as anyone is near me, his personality disturbs my self-complacency and restricts my freedom. In twenty-four hours I begin to hate the best of men; one because he is too long over his dinner; one because he has a cold and keeps blowing his nose. I become hostile to people the moment they come close to me, but it has always happened that the more I detest men individually, the more ardent becomes my love of humanity."

Surpassing these four inferior kinds of love is *Christian* love summarized in the words of Our Saviour: "A new commandment I give unto you that you love one another as I have loved you." What is new about this Commandment? Did not the Old Law say, "Love one another"? Have not all ethical teachers through the centuries pleaded for altruism? What is new about it? Two things are new: first, the way Our Lord loved us, that is, to a point of self-sacrifice. Second, it is new, because it is a Commandment. By making it a Commandment, Our Divine Lord made a distinction between liking and loving. Liking is in the emotions, in the temperament, in the glands, in feelings, and over these we have little or no control. Loving, however, is in the will and, therefore, is subject to command. There are certain things we do not like, and we cannot help not liking them. For example, some do not like fat women in tweeds; others cannot bear olives at the bottom of Martini glasses. I do not like chicken. Instinctive reactions in us we cannot completely control, but by putting love in the will, we can control it, and even extend it to those whom we do not like. Love, then, is not a gush but a virtue; not a spasmodic enthusiasm, but an abiding relationship of service, affection, and sacrifice.

The Commandment is new, not only because it is in the will, but also because the Model of such love is God Himself: "As I have loved you." He loved us when as yet we were sinners. When anyone does us wrong, we say, "You lost my love; change, and then I will love you." Our Blessed Lord, on the contrary, says, "Love someone, and then he will change. Let your love be the creation of his betterment." It was the love that He gave Peter the night that Peter denied Him that made Peter change. Tradition has it that Peter went out and wept so much that he created furrows in his cheeks, because he had hurt Someone that he loved.

Our Blessed Lord gave the test of love when He said, "Love your enemies." We are not to expect anything in return, but to go on loving even in the midst of hostility and persecution. Love is disinterested when it continues despite hate. By making the love of neighbor an affair of the will, and not a matter of feeling, Our Saviour took love out of the narrow circle of self, exiled it from the "I" castle, and set it fully on the side of the other person. He urged that we so efface self that we care for the other person for *his* sake alone and not for any ulterior purpose. We cross over the chasm and become the other person's possession. One way of knowing whether our love is totally disinterested is to compare it with the love we have for those who are dead. Here is absolutely no possibility of requital, return of friendship, pleasure, or utility. When love persists even without a return of love, then is the affection pure. Nature bids us be mindful of others; Christ bids us to put love where we do not find it, and thus will we find everyone lovable.

CHAPTER TWELVE

Why Some Become Communists

Why do some American people become Communists? One of the reasons most often given is that Communists are made by bad economic conditions. That is not true. Low economic standards are merely a *condition* of Communism, but they are not a *cause*. The *cause* of light in a room is the sun. The window is the *condition* of the light coming in. Bad economic conditions are not the cause of people becoming Communistic; if they were, countries with low economic standards would be most Communistic. The economic level of Burma is very low, but the people are definitely anti-Communist. Economic standards of Portugal and Ireland are not nearly so high as in the United States; yet both countries are definitely anti-Communist.

Furthermore, many who become Communists in the United States are those who belong to the middle class or even the rich. Juvenile delinquency also predominates in those same classes. Marx himself did not become a Communist because of his poverty; actually his father belonged to the middle class and sent him through the university. Marx was first an atheist, then a Communist. Economic conditions in the Garden of Paradise were excellent, but the first Red got in.

One reason why some become Communists is a reaction against liberalism. Liberalism can mean one of three things. First, it can mean that particular philosophy of the last century which believed that economic production should be uncontrolled by state, morality, or religion. Such was the liberalism of Adam Smith, John Stuart Mill, and the Manchester school.

But liberalism can also mean a belief in fundamental rights and liberties within the law. Every American is that kind of liberal. Such liberalism believes that everybody should be free to draw a triangle on condition that he give it three sides. It believes that everyone should be free to draw a giraffe on condition that he give it a long neck, for such is the nature of a giraffe. It believes that everyone should be free to drive his car in traffic, but on condition that he obey the traffic laws. This is the right kind of liberalism—freedom under the law.

Finally, liberalism can mean liberty without law. This is the kind of liberalism that makes Communists. Liberals of this variety are interested only in freedom *from* something, but not in freedom *for* something. They say they have an open mind, but it never closes on anything. They say they are looking for truth; yet if they ever met truth, they would drop dead. The reason they do not want Truth or Goodness or an Absolute is because the discovery of truth would commit them to responsibility. They are always unprepared for truth, like the golfer who in his first trip to the course makes a hole in one.

How does this kind of liberalism prepare for Communism?

According to this kind of liberalism, life has no purpose or final goal. Therefore, life is meaningless. But as soon as life becomes meaningless, the mind becomes revolutionary. A boiler has a purpose, imposed by the mind of an engineer, to contain steam at a given temperature. When it loses its purpose, it explodes. When persons reject the normal pattern of human life, given by God, they revolt. The present revolutionary tendency in youth in the world is not due to the fact that youth itself is perverse. The revolutionary character of modern youth throughout the world is due to a rightful protest against parents and educators who have not bequeathed to them the meaning of existence. In reaction against an irrational, unpurposeful existence, they seek compensation in the *intensity* of an experience such as sex license, revolution, or Communism.

Under this false theory of liberty, which is more correctly, license, everyone seeks to satisfy his own will. Continuous self-affirmation not only produces antagonisms between individuals, but conflict between classes. The logic of license is frightening. If all things are allowable, then man becomes a slave to his own freedom. After a while people tire of their freedom, because freedom rightfully implies responsibility. Then comes the reaction. Chaos becomes so general that fatigued minds look for someone to whom they can surrender their freedom and therefore their responsibility. This is Communism, which is the compulsory organization of the chaos created by a false liberalism. If there be no truth, there is nothing left but the forcible massing of individuals into social "happiness." Thus does boundless liberty lead to tyranny.

EVERYONE
SEEKING HIS
OWN WILL

COMMUNISM
ORGANIZES
THE CHAOS

If the sheep will not go into the sheepfold, dogs are sent after them to drive them in. "Goodness" of a new kind is achieved by necessity.

Klaus Fuchs, who passed atomic secrets to Russia, explained his Communism: "I had the sense of becoming a 'free man' because I succeeded in establishing myself completely independent of surrounding forces of society. Looking back on it, the best way of expressing it is to call it a controlled schizophrenia." Louis Budenz, the former editor of the Communist daily in the United States, calls Communists "men without faces." No longer self-determined, the party imposes its reason on them, rules their existence, and even tells them how to interpret history. Religious conversion deepens personal responsibility; Communist perversion destroys it.

Another reason why some become Communists is to escape a sense of guilt. Every man who does wrong has an uneasy conscience. This sense of guilt and uneasiness can come from bad behavior, such as dishonesty, pride, egotism, selfishness, lust, and alcoholism. But it can also come from having too much money.

A man whose conscience bothers him because he is not living right may eventually reach a point where he will say, "I want to escape this remorse and gnawing guilt. I find that all the defenders of morality, decency, and religion are deepening my guilty feeling. I hate them for doing so, but what can I do alone? The great advantage of Communism is that it will give my hate a collective status. Communism does away with distinctions of right or wrong; it even makes the wrong right and the right wrong. By joining the Communists I can solace my conscience by being interested in social justice. Then I will be righting everyone else's life, and Communism will let me lead my life as I please."

Educators in a democracy must be sure that the youth are taught to lead moral lives, for Communism makes progress in relation to the breakdown of morals. It even seeks to destroy morality in youth through the spread of false opinions and evil literature. Once a sense of justice is destroyed in the individual, Communists seek to get youth interested in what they call "social justice," that its *evil* may seem to be righteous.

Others have an uneasy conscience because they are rich. Perhaps their wealth was not acquired honestly; maybe it was, but they now see a tremendous disproportion between what they have and what others have, and they begin to feel uncomfortable. Their reaction may be twofold: either, to support Communism to salve their guilty conscience, or else to support it in the hope that "when the Revolution comes," they may keep their wealth. Communism has the great "advantage" of reforming everybody else, while leaving the self "free" for its own sin. Poor fools! Lenin said they are the first to be liquidated when Communism comes into power.

A third reason for Communism is to be found in the betrayal of the intelligentsia. A distinction is made between the intelligentsia and the intellectuals. The intelligentsia are those who have been educated beyond their intelligence. We are not speaking of people who are truly intellectual, who are necessary for culture and civilization. To be an intellectual is one of the noblest vocations God has given to man; teachers are the bearers of the Word, and "those who instruct shall shine as stars for all eternity." Few joys are greater than to mold young minds and young wills in the way of truth and goodness.

The word "intelligentsia" has a Latin root *intellectus* with a Russian ending *-sia*. In modern terms, it is Bolshevism tacked on to Western ideas, or vice versa. Generally, it is the Western that is absorbed into the Soviet. Arnold Toynbee says the intelligentsia are born to be unhappy, because there is something alien or hybrid in their make-up.

Fifty years ago there was such a thing as "economic slumming," in which the rich went down to the dives and cafés of the poor, not to relieve their needs by a surrender of their wealth, but in order to enjoy the shock and the thrill of riches contrasted with poverty.

Economic slumming today has become intellectual slumming, under which the intelligentsia go down to the Communist masses, not to give them the truth of which they are the custodians, but in order to enjoy the shock and the thrill of mass revolutionary movements without intelligent direction.

The intelligentsia are uprooted. They are not at home in a culture; uprooted spiritually and morally disoriented, they fit into Western Christian civilization like a woman trying to get a 7 foot into a 3-A shoe. That is why many of the intelligentsia no longer write books in their own native countries; some Americans expatriate themselves to write in England, others in France, others in Spain, others in Africa; some Irishmen go to England to expound their ideas, and some of the German intelligentsia to America. These men are not at home at home; they feel the need of an alien class to act as a transformer of their ideas, that is, to change them from low to high voltage. Because they have lost their roots and their culture, they gravitate to Bolshevism or what is alien to the great tradition that has made Western civilization and democracy. The so-called "wise" men are not so wise as they think they are.

There is no danger whatever to academic freedom when a professor is asked by his government if he is a member of the Communist party. But there is danger to academic freedom when a professor uses American liberty by invoking the Constitution in order to destroy it and deliver us over to Moscow. Despite moral failings, which helps make Communists, it must never be forgotten that the grace of God can undo Communism and make them free men again. Such was the case of Douglas Hyde, the editor of the London Communist daily, and his wife. Both were listening one night to the radio as Vishinsky was speaking. Mrs. Hyde, after listening to him for ten minutes, became exasperated. Dashing to the radio, she shut off Vishinsky, saying, "I am getting sick and tired of Vishinsky. He is talking about peace, but he is doing everything possible to obstruct and destroy it. I do not believe he wants peace." And with that, her husband said, "You are not talking as a Communist." She said, "I don't care whether I am talking as a Communist or not." He retorted, "If you do not stop that kind of talk, I will report you to the party and you will be disciplined." She said, "All right. Report me." "Why," he said, "you are beginning to talk as if you might go into the Church." She said, "I am." He said, "Shake, so am I." God can do His work when we put ourselves on His side.

CHAPTER THIRTEEN

Nice People

This subject can be introduced by the story of the egotist who went to see a physician, complaining of a headache. The doctor, upon examination, asked, "Do you feel a distressing pain in the forehead?" "Yes," said the patient. "And a rather throbbing pain in the back of the head?" "Yes." "And piercing pains here at the side?" "Yes." The doctor explained: "Your halo is on too tight."

The point is that almost everyone today believes that he has a halo. If it does not come from virtue, at least it comes from a shampoo. Mark Twain once said, "When I reflect upon the number of disagreeable people who I am told have gone to a better world, I am moved to lead a different life."

A distinction must be made between "nice" people and "awful" people.

The nice people *think* they are good; the awful people *know* they are not. The nice people never believe they do wrong, or break a commandment, or are guilty of any infraction of the moral law. If they do anything that reason would call wrong, they have various ways of explaining it away. Goodness

is always their own, but badness is due to something outside of themselves. Some say that it is due to economic circumstances: one will say, "I was born too rich" and another, "I was born too poor." Psychology also comes in handy to explain away their faults, for example, "I have an Oedipus complex" or an "Electra complex," or "I have an inferiority complex."

The awful people, on the contrary, generally are not rich enough to be psychoanalyzed; they have never been introduced to their subconscious, and they think themselves just plain bad. Nice people, if they are guilty of intemperance, will call themselves alcoholics. Awful people call themselves drunkards—sometimes just plain "bums." The nice people say they have a disease. The drunkards say, "I am a no-good." The nice people judge themselves by the vices from which they abstain; the awful people judge themselves by the virtues from which they have fallen. When a nice person sees another doing something that he regards as wrong, he criticizes; when an awful

person sees a man going to death on a scaffold, he says with
St. Philip Neri, "There go I but for the grace of God." When a
nice person really sins, he says, "What a fool I am." When an
awful person really sins, he says, "What a sinner I am."

The nice people always follow the ethics of social ortho-
doxy, or convention. They lose less sleep over falsifying an
income-tax return than over wearing a white tie instead of
a black one at a banquet or are more scandalized at a preacher's
grammatical errors than at his false doctrine. Refinement and
respectability form a large concept in his goodness, and social
convention is given the force of a Divine Command; what is
respectable or usual is not wrong. Living in a society where
divorces are common, the nice people say, "Well, everybody
is doing it; therefore, divorce is right." The nice people think
they are going straight because they are traveling in the best
circles; the awful people are those whose vices are open and
who are generally below the level of social convention. When
nice people break all the commandments of God, their friends
say that "she is so nice" or "he is so nice"; when the awful people break a few of the Commandments in a grosser way, they
are labeled "low and unrefined." Nice people love to read
scandals about nasty people because it makes them feel so good.
In truth, the nice people are those whose sins have not been
found out, the awful people are those whose sins have been
found out.

Society has no place either for those who are too good
or for those who are too bad. It is only the mediocre who sur-

vive. That is why on the Hill of Calvary Our Lord was crucified with two thieves. They were too bad for conventional
morality; Our Lord was too good. Often during His lifetime,
Our Lord always associated with "those awful people." He
tells the story of the prodigal son who was preferred before his
virtuous brother. He praises a son who rebelled and repented,
rather than the one who professed loyalty and then failed. He
rejoices in the lost sheep that was found and the lost coin that
was recovered, because the Gospel that He preached was not
a condemnation of obvious badness, but rather a condemnation
of obvious goodness.

One of the beautiful incidents in His life is concerned with
the nice people and the awful people. It happened after Our
Blessed Lord had spent a night in prayer in the Garden of
Olives and then came early in the morning to the Temple on
the occasion of the great Feast of the Tabernacle. As tens of
thousands of people gathered into the city, it was not unlikely
that, in the joy of the feast, there might be one or the other
instance of excess, or a gross violation of morality.

In any case, the very nice people, the Scribes and Pharisees,
found a woman whom they had caught in the act of adultery.
It was interesting that they had caught her in the act, and that
they were not so much moved by the horror of the sin, but
rather by a desire to catch and ensnare Our Lord in His speech.
Dragging her from seclusion, they brought her to the sacred
precincts of the Temple, subjecting the unveiled, disheveled,
terror-stricken woman to the cold and sensual curiosity of
their malicious associates.

The charge against the woman was put in such a fashion as to accuse Him, rather than her, and to make it appear that either He was violating the law of Moses, or the law of the Romans who had conquered their country. They began saying, "The law of Moses commands that this woman be stoned to death. What sayest Thou?" It was true that the law of Moses did order the stoning of such a woman, for suggestions of this kind are found in Deuteronomy and Leviticus. But that law was now a dead letter. They were practically saying to Our Lord, "You say that you come from God, that you are the Son of God. Well, the law of Moses comes from God. If you come from God and the law of Moses comes from God, then order that this woman be stoned. Put her to death."

But this was only half their trick. For some decades, ever since the Romans had been masters of their country, only the Roman authorities could put anyone to death. If, therefore, He ordered the woman stoned in obedience to the law of Moses, they would report Him to Pontius Pilate, who, in turn, would accuse Him of violating a law of Caesar.

In either case, they thought He was caught. If He stoned the woman to death, He would be guilty of treason against Caesar; if He released the woman, He would be guilty of heresy against Moses. It was a kind of dilemma of justice and mercy. If He condemned the woman, He would not be merciful, and He claimed that He was merciful; if He released the woman, He would not be just, and He claimed that He was just.

In answer to the dilemma, Our Blessed Lord leaned forward and moved His finger over the dust that was on the Temple floor. It was the only time in His life He ever wrote. What did He write? We do not know what He wrote, but we do know that He leaned over twice and twice scribbled something in the dust. It is our guess that the first time He wrote in the dust the sins of the woman, and a gentle breeze seemed to come up suddenly to blow the writing away.

As He wrote, they persisted in their questions: "What sayest Thou about the law of Moses?" He looked up at them and gave the answer: "Let him who is without sin cast the first stone." He was not abrogating the law of Moses. He was demanding a new jury; He was asking if that woman could fittingly be judged by those who have committed counter-sins. She had too much passion; they had too little. She was sinning from an excessive love, they from a defect. New executioners were being summoned for the Mosaic dispensation. He proclaimed that only the innocent had the right to condemn, and He, Who was Innocence Itself, would not condemn her, because He was going to die one day for her and for all other sinners.

Having heard His words, the nice people looked at one another to see if one of them would be brave enough to say that he was not guilty of any sin. None of them left. Our Lord leaned over again and wrote—and this time it is our belief that He wrote the sins of all of the nice people—the sins that had not yet been found out. As they saw their sins exposed to the public gaze, they began leaving one by one, beginning with the eldest. And only three were left. One can picture Our Blessed Lord looking up at one of them with one of those deep,

penetrating glances that anticipate judgment, then writing in
the dust. This time where there was no wind to blow the accusation away. He wrote: "Thief." The nice man dropped his
stone and left. Looking at the second Pharisee and reading his
soul, He wrote: "Murderer." He dropped his stone and left.
There was only one left—the youngest and the boldest of all.
He had already taken the stone from a neighbor's hand,
weighed it to see whether it was heavier than the one he possessed; then he had returned the lighter stone to keep the heavier one to throw at the woman. Our Lord looked him in the
eye, knew his sin, and wrote for the third time: "Adulterer."
He quickly dropped his stone and fled.

Now only the sinner and Our Lord were left: *miseria et
misericordia*, misery and mercy, pitiableness and pity. Addressing her with the title He had once given His Mother at
Cana, and would give her once again at the Cross, He said,
"Woman, where are they who accuse thee." She said, "They
are not here, my Lord." He answered, "Neither will I accuse
thee. Go and sin no more."

He was not making light of her sin, because the time was
not far distant when He would have to pay for it on the Cross.
What He was doing was convicting the nice people of their
sins and asking, "Are there no poor around their gates unfed,
no sick untended, and no souls untaught?" "Let him who is
without sin cast the first stone." Was not their own passion-
lessness responsible for that woman's passion, their own neg-
lect of the poor the contributing cause of her vice? What a
pity that those nice people did not know anything about the

Oedipus complex! They could have said that a "mother complex" was responsible for their behavior. The nice people, convicted by their own conscience, leave Him. The nasty people, symbolized by the woman, remain. The awful people who do remain, He exhorts to break not only from a particular sin but from all sin.

The nice people do not find God, because, denying personal guilt, they have no need of a Redeemer. The awful people, who are passionate, sensual, warped, lonely, weak, but who nevertheless make an attempt at goodness, are quick to realize that they need another help than their own; that they cannot lift themselves by their own bootstraps. Their sins create an emptiness. From that point on, like the woman taken in sin, it is "Christ or nothing."

What surprises there will be on the Last Day when the awful people are found in the Kingdom of Heaven: "The harlots and the publicans will enter the Kingdom of Heaven before the Scribes and the Pharisees." The surprises will be threefold: first, because we are going to see a number of people there whom we never expected to see. Of some of them will we say, "How did he get here? Glory be to God, look at her!" The second surprise will be not seeing a number of the nice people whom we expected to see. But these surprises will be mild compared with the third and greatest surprise of all, and that surprise will be that we are there.

CHAPTER FOURTEEN

Why Work Is Boring

Jerome K. Jerome once said, "Work positively fascinates me. I could sit and look at it all day."

The nature of work. An animal works; for example, we speak of "working like a beaver" or being "busy as a bee." The work of man and beast are alike in that both produce results: for example, a bee produces honey; man, a work of art. But there is also a difference. In man there is an intention. Man has reason and will. Being made to the image of God, he leaves the impress of his reason on what he does. An animal operates only by instinct, not by freedom and thought, intention and purpose, as man does. Thus in all work there are two elements: the result produced and the human intention or purpose, which includes self-perfection or development. In the building of a cathedral, stones are cut and placed; such is the result produced. But there is also the intention, namely, to honor and glorify God. Michelangelo produced a marvelous statue of Moses. His intention was to glorify the great Mosaic Lawgiver. When he finished the statue, he felt it was so perfect, he took his chisel and struck the base of it, saying, "Speak."

A farmer produces results, namely, his crops. His intention may be to intensify his knowledge of farming, to live virtuously, to aid the common good, or just to make money.

How the Dignity of Work Is Lost. Industrial work is a little different; much of it is boring. There is soul-destroying repetition and routine that anesthetizes in the screwing of a bulb on a machine as the conveyor belt passes by. Year after year, identically the same detail is fulfilled. Results are produced, but the intention—the development of personality, the production of social good—is almost lost. A man begins to feel, "I work in order to live; not to perfect myself or express my creativeness or my individuality." All some can say is, "I put a nut on a bolt that goes into the spring, that goes into the

chassis, that goes into the auto; when the auto is finished, it is pretty hard to see what I have done." Uncreative work is repellent, because impersonal. Work is so specialized that

workers today are like hens who lay eggs only to have them
put into an incubator. They never have the thrill of raising
their chicks.

Two bad effects flow from routine labor, particularly
mechanized labor. The first effect is, it is boring. Man loves
to express his individuality simply because he is different from
any other man in the world. Whether it be planting a garden,
whittling wood, or collecting butterflies, he likes to see the
imprint of his character on what he does. Having within himself the image of God, he wants in his turn to put his image on
matter. When he does the same thing over and over again,
his personality is denied expression. A tension is created within
himself between his natural desire for individual expression
of his work and the standardized, impersonal, and mechanized
things he is called upon to do. No wonder people are sick and
tired of it! They feel that all they do when they work is to
make money in order that they may eat, and then eat in order
that they may have strength to go back to work again.

Another effect of repetitious, dull work is that it subordinates the spirit of man to the economic and the mechanical.
Man's freedom comes in contact with necessity. He sees
himself as serving production, instead of production serving
him. He who is meant to be the master, becomes the slave.
Man does not exist for the sake of production, but production
exists for the sake of man, just as man is not to be understood
in terms of sex, but sex is to be understood in terms of man.
If a father has eleven children but enough money to buy only
ten hats, should he cut off the head of the eleventh child? If

economics were primary, that would be the logic. Coffee is
thrown into the ocean, milk poured on the ground, grain
stored, bananas thrown into the sea, while two-thirds of the
people of the world are going to bed hungry every night. And
why? Because the maintenance of an economic price has become more important than human life.

The growth of the revolutionary spirit among workers
is not always due to Communism. It is often the workers' rightful protest against the defacement of the Divine Image within
them, because they know that, being the noblest creatures on
earth, they may not be degraded to the order of chemicals,
matter, and economics.

Man is gradually coming under the control of impersonal
human forces. Once capital was anonymous in the sense that
the responsibility for conditions was hidden; now labor, in
some instances, is becoming anonymous inasmuch as one dare
not act against those who control it.

Communism is the final logic of the dehumanization of man.
The industrial civilization of the Western world has no intent
to destroy man's freedom, nor to deny his personality. But
Communism does. Denying God, it reduces man to a robot.
Denying Spirit, man no longer has a right to impress his personality on things. He has no personality; he is a tool of the
state, a mechanized ant in the anthill of the Soviet state. Produce! Produce! Produce! Man, under Communism, has no
other reason for existing.

Dostoievski in the last century saw Communism coming
to his beloved Russia. In one of his great works, *The Brothers*

Karamazov, he pictures the Devil bargaining again with Christ about turning stones into bread. Satan describes how, under his regime, millions will follow him because they are ready to surrender their freedom for bread or "security." Under any other system, man might refuse bread, if it were the condition of losing his liberty; but, under Communism, "security" is more important than liberty.

The Devil says to Christ, "We shall persuade them that they will only become free when they renounce their freedom to us and submit to us. Turn those stones into bread and mankind will run after Thee, Christ, like a flock of sheep, grateful and obedient and forever trembling lest Thou withdraw Thy Hand and deny them bread. Dost Thou not know, O Christ, that the ages will pass, and humanity will proclaim by the lips of their sages that there is no crime, there is no sin, there is only hunger. Now, those days are on us now. In the end they will lay their freedom at our feet and say to us, 'Make us slaves but feed us.' In their leisure hours we shall make their life like a child's game, with children's songs and innocent dances. We shall even allow them their sins, and they will love us like children because we allow them their sins. We shall allow them or forbid them to live with their wives or their mistresses, to have or have not children according to whether they have been obedient or disobedient to us, and they will submit to us. What I say to Thee, O Christ, will come to pass, and our dominion will be built up over the world. I repeat: tomorrow, Thou, Christ, shalt see the obedient flock at a sign from me, hasten to heap hot cinders about the pile where I will burn

Thee for coming to hinder us, for if anyone has ever deserved our fires, it is Thou. Tomorrow I shall burn Thee. *Dixi*—I have spoken."

If mechanized work makes it hard to put one's own intention or purpose to work, and if Communism completely destroys purpose, personality, and freedom, are we to conclude that an industrial civilization is evil? Certainly not! Rather is it a blessing, and much happiness would be lost to this world if we did away with all our technological progress.

How the Dignity of Work May Be Restored. Instead of doing away with mechanized civilization, we need only take away its defects through an economic and a spiritual remedy. The economic remedy is to dignify the worker by restoring his responsibility, and by making him feel that he is contributing to something that is his own. This will be done by capital giving the workers some share in the profits or management or ownership of industry. Not all the profits; capital must have its just share. It might be well for the government to decrease excess-profits taxes, which are so often spent through bureaucracies, in order that this wealth which the workers helped produce be given directly to them. Workers are willing to sit down on someone else's tools, but they are not willing to sit down on their own. If capital contends they are not interested, it might be well to give them some capital to defend. One is often asked, "Are you for capital, or are you for labor?" The question is spurious to an honest mind. Capital and labor are classes, and no class is always right. We have suffered a great deal in the past from the evils of capital, and we could suffer a great deal from the evils of labor. Instead of being for either capital or labor, we should be for both. To ask, "Which is more important?" is like asking which is more important to a man, his right leg or his left. Both! Capital and labor work together, producing for the common good; let both be responsible, and both will have dignity, and the boredom will disappear.

The other remedy is spiritual. Mechanized work can be saved from drudgery by doing it with a Divine intention. We can do different things for different reasons, like dropping money in a cup just to be seen, or giving it simply because we see Christ in the poor. There is no work in the world that cannot be sanctified. Raising a microphone, making a table, sweeping floors, threading needles, working at the routine machines in airplane and automobile factories—all of these operations can be sanctified and made a prayer, provided they are offered up with a Divine intention. Whether we eat or drink or whatsoever we do, sanctification is possible when the task is offered in the name of God. We all have work to do that is unpleasant, but it becomes pleasant when we love someone. Work done for the love of God makes a man happier and gives him an inner peace the world cannot take away.

Our attitude toward capital and labor must be as impartial as that of Christ Himself. He was not just a carpenter; He was not just a poor man. Our Blessed Lord was a rich man who became poor: "being rich He became poor for your sakes." Our Blessed Lord was, as it were, a capitalist Who became a laborer. This Worker Who fixed the flat roofs of Nazarene homes was also the one from Whose finger tips tumbled planets and worlds. He Who labored in a carpenter shop was also the one Who carpentered the universe itself. He is the bond that will bring capital and labor together and restore the dignity of man. He is the only One in the world of Whom both capital and labor can say, "He came from our ranks. He is one of our own."

CHAPTER FIFTEEN

Man, the Captain of His Destiny

A boy was asked by his father to work out a jigsaw puzzle which was a map of the world. In an amazingly short time, the jigsaw puzzle was put together. The father said, "How did you know how to put this puzzle together? You do not know geography." The little boy answered, "On the other side was the puzzle of a man. So I put the man together, and the world came out all right."

If the world is to be remade, man must first be remade. Man does resemble, to some extent, lower creation. He is like the stones and the chemicals, inasmuch as he has existence; he is like the plants, inasmuch as he has vegetative powers of growth and nutrition; he is like the animals, inasmuch as he has emotions, passions, and also sense knowledge. But man is unique and is differentiated from all lower creation, because of his reason and will, which the lower creatures lack.

How this higher part of man, which is thinking and willing, works out in relationship to the lower can be explained by the following illustration.

The pilot on the top of the ship has a wheel which con-
nects through the ship with the engine room. Near the engine
is the boiler, into which waters come from the sea and pour
back again. The pilot steers the boat by the stars, *i.e.*, by fixed
norms which are outside himself, which enable him to work
incessantly toward his goal or purpose, namely, the port.

The pilot makes decisions, that is, he uses his free will,
thanks to the guidance of the stars and the port to which he
is sailing. All his decisions are communicated below to the
engine room. This stands for the subconscious, while the boiler
and the water that come into it from outside represent the
unconscious in man. To a great extent everything that happens
in the engine room (subconscious) and even the amount of
water that comes into the boiler from the sea (unconscious)
are determined by the pilot. The port stands for the eternal
destiny of man, which is happiness, or union with perfect Life
and Truth and Love, which is God. As the pilot has the heavens

to guide him, so does man have a conscience and other aids which reflect the moral law of God.

As the pilot does not determine his course independent of the heavens, neither does man determine his course subjectively. He has to have a law outside himself, as he sets his watch by something outside of the watch. Which notes are right on a piano? Are all the black notes right, and all the white notes wrong? Which notes are right and wrong is determined by the score, or the composition, which acts as the standard and determinative. In like manner, man has an ethical guide, the moral law of God, which helps him arrive at his port.

The pilot could, if he wished, make bad decisions; as a result of those bad decisions, the machinery might get out of order and the boiler become clogged. But man can become more clogged than any machine. This clogging of modern man is a result of several denials of his true nature, for example:

1. There is no port, no eternal destiny; life is meaningless.
2. There is no moral law; man is his own guide.
3. Reason and will are not important, because man is not responsible for his actions.

Modern psychology first lost its soul, then its reason, and now it is losing its consciousness. As a result, it is fashionable to say he cannot be guilty, because he is not responsible.

As a result, it is claimed that, if you are to understand man, you must study his unconsciousness. What is in his unconsciousness, it is said, to a great extent comes from prenatal influence or the way the parents conducted themselves toward the child; but the child himself is not accountable.

If we applied this silly idea to the ship which began sinking, as modern man is sinking, this is the way a particular brand of psychologists would approach the problem: "If you want to find out why that ship sank, analyze the waters that pour into that boiler. Put that boiler on a couch! Analyze the chemistry of its waters; discover what ancient salts went into their composition; from what part of the sea they come; against what shores they washed. Maybe the waters came from the sea called an 'Oedipus complex,' or maybe the waters that got into the boiler came from a river that was called an 'Electra complex.' Maybe they became clogged with the flotsam and the jetsam of religious morality, faith, morals, totems, and taboos."

A more rational approach to the problem would be to question the pilot, instead of analyzing the waters. Maybe the pilot was drunk; maybe he refused to follow the chart; perhaps he deliberately changed his course.

The difference between the two methods can be illustrated by turning the picture of the ship upside down. What is important in the ship, namely, the pilot, and in man, namely, his reason and will, are now at the bottom and least important place, and what is secondary is made primary. No wonder man is shipwrecked!

In criticizing this distorted view of man, it must be remembered:

1. This is not a criticism of psychiatry.
2. This is not a criticism of the psychoanalytic method, which is very valid and which is at times very necessary.

There are many pathological or abnormal cases where the subconsciousness or unconscious must be analyzed, but it is quite wrong to universalize the *method* that is used in *pathological* cases to make it a *philosophy* for *normal* people.

As the great psychiatrist, C. J. Jung, has explained:

Modern man is somehow fascinated by only pathological manifestations of the unconscious mind. Freud himself, the founder of psychoanalysis, has thrown a glaring light upon the dirt, the darkness and the evil of the psychic hinterland and has presented these things as so much refuse and slag. It has awakened in many people an admiration for all this filth. The unexpected result of the spiritual change is that an uglier face has been put upon the world. The kind of psychology Freud and Adler represent leaves out the spirit and is suited to people who believe they have no spiritual need and no spiritual aspiration. In this matter both the doctor and the patient deceive themselves because of their exclusive concern with drives and they fail to satisfy the inner needs of the patient. A psychoneurosis must be understood as a suffering of a human being who had not discovered what life means.

Freud is interested only in the casual interpretation of sexual symptoms. He completely overlooks the fact that in certain cases the supposed causes of the neuroses were always present but have no pathological effect until a disturbance of the conscious attitude set in and led to a neurotic upset. Disturbances in the sphere of unconscious drive are not primary but secondary phenomena.

What is primary is what happens to a man's thoughts, his choices, his decisions, his resolutions, and his character; man is what he makes himself, not what his grandfather or grandmother made him.

Much that is in the subconscious or unconscious is there, certainly, because the consciousness, or the higher part of man, repressed it. But why did consciousness want to repress it? Why does a gunman want to conceal the evidence that will convict him or throw the body into the river? The reason man wants to repress many ideas is because they are violations of the moral order and his conscience. Rather than face his guilt, he becomes a coward or an escapist.

Jung concludes:

When conscious life has lost its meaning and its promise, it is as though a panic had broken loose and we heard the explanation, "Let us eat, drink and be merry for tomorrow we die."

Denying personal guilt, responsibility, and the need of amendment, modern man seeks to project his guilt either *outside* or *below*. If he projects guilt outside of himself, he blames it on somebody else. If he pushes it below into the cellar of his mind, he becomes less and less aware of his real self. This projection is like a shadow. Suppose hundreds of thousands deny the God-given faculties of reason and will, and affirm that their characters are made by some irresponsible, dark, covetous, libidinous forces—then there is created the Great Shadow. This Shadow is denied responsibility or unrecognized guilt; in a word, it is projected Evil.

But if Evil is *outside* man, then does it not follow that society or evil "social forces" must be reformed, but not man? So long as man recognizes responsibility for his deeds, then society can be remade by remaking man. But if the shadow is allowed to grow bigger and bigger, it will not be long before people say, "We want a leader for the shadow. We want a captain for that evil thing! We want that which has divested us of all responsibility to have a personality all its own"—that is how slave states and dictators are born.

The distance is not great between the point where human beings deny they are responsible and the point where they throw themselves down before a philosophy which explains away all freedom and all responsibility, which is Communism. Dostoievski warned us, "The time will come when men will say there is no guilt, there is no sin, there is no crime; there is only hunger. Men will come crawling to the feet of a dictator and say, 'Take our freedom. Give us bread.' " The denial of personal guilt makes men ready to surrender their liberty. Better is it for man to realize he has evil tendencies which must be fought and combated in order that his higher self may emerge.

CHAPTER SIXTEEN

The Liberation of Sex

Whenever a movie appears or a book is published, based on breaking one of the Commandments of God, there are not wanting those who justify it by saying, "At last the subject of sex has been brought out into the open. We had to wait for this enlightened twentieth century for a book or a movie which has liberated sex."

What is meant by "liberation of sex"? Liberation from what? Liberation could be from three things:

1. Liberation from privacy.
2. Liberation of the part from the whole.
3. Liberation from law and order.

If it means any of these three, it is not real liberation.

1. *Liberation from privacy.* There are certain things that every person likes to do by himself; for example, a woman likes to weigh herself alone. That is why the numbers in a weighing machine are printed in small type. Because privacy is sacred,

every person wants to blow his own nose. When we are children, mothers get hold of our noses with the injunction, "Blow hard." A day finally comes in the life of every boy when he resents it; on that day he can say, "Today, I am a man." When he objects to the intrusion of his privacy, he comes to a recognition that he is a personality and that there are certain inviolable rights associated with it which make him rebel against spying and meddling. But today there are those who contend, "Nobody has ever brought this subject of nose blowing before the public. Too long has it been kept behind closed doors. Why not liberate this subject? Let's blow it wide open! Why not have a Kleenex report on nose blowing? The dark ages are past when a person had a right to do things by himself without a public investigator inquiring how he blew his nose." It may be very true that during the Victorian days it was common for people to say that man had no nose; perhaps our error today is to believe that is all anyone has. We are speaking of noses, but it is easy to make the application to other subjects.

Suppose a husband and wife embraced one another at 42d and Broadway. There is nothing wrong about the affection; nothing unethical. But why does everyone feel very differently about a husband and wife embracing at 42d and Broadway and a husband and wife eating out of doors in a park? The difference is this: certain actions between people are personal, intimate, and incommunicable, and to make them common or public is to make them vulgar; therefore, to prostitute them. Everyone has a key to his own front door and to his own home. Those who have respect for their personalities in a moral and righteous way resent investigators having a passkey to their homes.

"Liberation" in the sense of destroying personal privileges is the language of tyranny. Communists speak of the "liberation" of Poland. They boast that they have "liberated" China. What do they mean by liberating China, liberating Poland or any other country? They mean depriving people of their personal rights and the right to lead their own lives. Those who would destroy decency and morality are also in favor of that kind of "liberation," but such "liberation" is in truth slavery, decay, and chaos.

This innate regard for the sacredness of love explains timidity in a woman which makes her shrink from a too precocious revelation and surrender of the secret of her creative power. If she does like to talk about it publicly, she has lost the mystery of life. It also explains chivalry in man toward woman, not because he believes her to be physically weaker, but because of the awe he feels in the presence of mystery.

People are not prudes because they keep the uniqueness of the secret to themselves; monkeys are not "liberated" because they do not keep the secret. Monkeys are not persons, and therefore they lack the communication, not of a glandular reflex, but the secret of a heart. The stud farm is not the same as the hearth and home.

2. *Liberation of the part from the whole.* Man is a composite creature, made up of body and soul. He has instincts and emotions like an animal, but he also has a spirit which is very un-animal. Because man has a reason and a will, it follows

that no experience which man has seemingly in common with
the animal will be exactly the same as it is in the animal. Digestion in a horse is not the same as digestion in a man. Physio-
logically, there is a resemblance, but because man has a mind
and can worry and plan for the future, he can also have ulcers.
Chickens never have ulcers. To isolate one faculty or experience from the whole man, such as the isolation of sex, is to mis-
understand sex. There is a world of difference between sex
in pigs and love in humans.

Picture an orchestra leader who suddenly became very conscious of his hands. They seem like hams at his side. He picks

up a baton, but feels that everybody is looking at his hands.
Have you ever noticed that on television and in the theater,
hardly anybody knows any more what to do with his hands?
As soon as the performers come out, they have to light a ciga-
rette. That keeps them busy for a while. If this orchestra leader

were conscious only of his hands, he would not be able to direct an orchestra. But if he became absorbed in the music and the score he had to direct, his hands would act normally and he would be very unconscious of them. If a singer is conscious of his larynx, he cannot sing. As Oscar Wilde said, "Every detail is vulgar."

Those who "liberate" sex, in the sense of separating it from the rational nature of man, are making it vulgar. The larynx in a man is not the same as the larynx in a lynx. The behavior of the two will be different because the composite is different. The fallacy of interpreting man in terms of sex is obviously wrong, for it is man as a composite of body and soul that explains sex. G. K. Chesterton has given us a beautiful satire on those who would interpret every dream, every action and desire, in terms of sex. Chesterton satirizes this by suggesting we interpret everything in terms of beer.

The whole life of a child of either sex is actuated by beer. The first action of which a child is capable is a lusty yell. We have established the fact that this is a cry for beer or, at any rate, for some kind of drink. If the child does not drink beer, it is because his system is not yet capable of drinking beer, but behind the relish for milk is the desire for beer. These we call primary instincts. Now, the secondary instincts are to be found in the love of popping corks, of yellow-brown colors, of frothy substances like soap and so on. The child instinctively calls his father "papa," which resembles the popping of a cork, and his mother "mama." He still calls his mother "mama" which gives the noise of a liquid being poured into a glass. All the gurgling noises of childhood go to prove the strength of this instinct. Most of our knowledge is based upon dreams which we have established as the most reliable evidence possible. We know by means too long to tell you here that even very young people dream of beer. They dream of nothing else. When a child dreams of a boat upon a lake, what is that but a symbol of beer? A shower of rain, a river or sea, everything yellow or brown is beer. Everything in something else is beer. A nut in a shell, for example, is obviously representative of beer in a bottle. Everything issuing from an aperture is beer. Everything that moves is beer, particularly quick-moving, jerky things which are reminiscent of hops. In fact, we may say a child cannot dream of anything but beer.

3. *Liberation from law and order.* One of the differences between man and the beast is that man talks and an animal cannot. Speech requires ideas, reason, and a knowledge, purpose, goals, choices, and signification, all of which are wanting to the beast. To preserve the reason that there is in speech, there are laws of grammar, rhetoric, and syntax. One of the laws is that every sentence shall have a subject, a predicate, and a verb. Has any fool yet arisen to plead for the "liberation from grammar"? We can imagine such a person arguing in somewhat the manner of those who are so glib about "liberation of sex":

"How long have you people been following the laws of grammar and speech? Why should you not decide for yourself how you will talk? Is it not about time to get away from these medieval dogmas, codes, and barriers which obstruct speech and tie it down to conventions? The Dark Ages believed that every sentence should have a subject, a predicate, and a verb. Are you still bound by such antiquated superstitions? Throw off these shackles! You have nothing to lose but your chains. Liberate speech from grammar, sense, and reason! The times are changing. We will send experts throughout the country to discover whether those who speak are still using subjects, predicates, and verbs. We will not send our experts to the professors of rhetoric and grammar and syntax in our universities and colleges. Certainly not! These people are 'reactionaries,' 'medieval,' 'Victorian.' We will send our investigators and our experts to the crazy house. We have already examined 8,843 crazy people. We know that there are 160 million people in the United States, but we want these 8,843 people to be a sample from which we can deduce statistics for the whole population. Our researchers have established that 72.96431 per cent of the people whom we have examined are using split infinitives; they split them wide open! We have discovered that 98.643756 per cent of the people whom we have examined are making propositions only with prepositions. We find that 75.39732164 per cent of the people are using only adjectives in sentences. Other statistics prove that some are merely using pronouns in sentences, many using singular verbs with plural subjects. That means that these people are making progress. They are throwing off the rules of grammar! Speech is liberated!"

It is very likely that people will one day say that the flag has no mystery or meaning in our American life, nor is it a symbol of a piety or sacred loyalty. Then someone will write an article on the "Liberation of the American Flag" and plead that it should not only be flown above our heads but trampled beneath our feet. To call that day "liberation" will be to take a worm's-eye view of America; the same tragedy could happen to love if one took a worm's-eye view of it.

In the midst of a great sea there was an island with a great wall, a high wall. On that island lived children, who sang, danced, and played. One day some men came to the island in a rowboat. They called themselves "liberators," and said to the children, "Who put up these walls? Who built up these barriers? Can you not see that they are restraining your freedom and your liberty? Tear them down. Be free." The children tore down the walls. Now if you go back, you will find all the children huddled together in the center of the island, afraid to sing, afraid to play, afraid to dance, afraid of falling into the sea!

CHAPTER SEVENTEEN

The Philosophy of Communism

Communism is not a political party because once it comes into power, it suppresses all other parties. As Molotov once said, "In Russia the Communist party is in power and all the other parties are in jail." Neither is Communism primarily an economic system. Economics is a superstructure on its philosophy of life. To understand this philosophy, one ought to know something about the life of Karl Marx, who gave Communism to the world—then something about its philosophy.

Karl Marx was born in the Rhineland of Germany on May 5, 1818, of a rather distinguished family; his father, a lawyer of considerable importance, was descended from a long line of rabbis. For political reasons, but not through conviction, the whole family joined a Christian sect. But after baptism no one in the family ever attended church or synagogue.

Young Karl went to the University of Bonn. When about eighteen years of age, he fell in love with Jennie von Westphalen, a companion of one of his sisters, who was about four years his senior. Later on when he left his "fairy princess," as he called her, to study philosophy at the University of Berlin, he filled the gap by writing poetry to her. During the seven years between the time he met Jennie and the time he married her, his poetry filled three volumes. All of that poetry has been lost! Some wish his philosophy had been lost and his poetry saved.

When Marx at twenty-five married Jennie, he stopped writing poetry. But during his honeymoon, he filled five copybooks full of extracts from Montesquieu, Rousseau, Machiavelli, and other political and social writers. This is a queer sort of man who writes poetry to his girl before he is married, and plunges into political philosophy during his honeymoon!

After marriage, he sojourned for a time in Belgium and France and then at the age of thirty-one went to England, where he lived the rest of his life. Six children were born to him, most of whom died early in life. Marx had two sources of income. One briefly came from his services as foreign correspondent for the *New York Tribune*. The other source of his income was his rich friend, Friedrich Engels, the son of a merchant in Manchester, England. Engels sent Marx about $1,750 a year. When Engels' common-law wife, Mary Burns, died, Engels took the death rather tragically. He wrote of his sadness to Marx, who answered, "I am sorry. Can you send me £15?" Engels, who collaborated with Marx in developing the philosophy of Communism, wrote this interesting response: "Karl, you found the moment well chosen to advertise the superiority of your cold philosophy." It should not be forgotten that Engels called it a "cold philosophy." It is easy to understand how a man who never earned his own living, but survived through the aid of others, should so readily develop a system of economics based on the dispossession of others.

Marx was a deep student and the proud possessor of a Ph.D. from the University of Jena. For many years, Marx spent from nine o'clock in the morning until seven at night at the British Museum gathering material for his book, *Das Kapital.* Jennie one day said to him, when she found it hard to pay all the bills, "Karl, if you had only spent a little more time making capital, instead of writing about it, we would have been far better off."

In 1883, Marx died shortly before his sixty-fifth birthday and was buried in Highgate Cemetery, London. Hardly a dozen persons were at the grave. The funeral oration was given by Friedrich Engels, who said that as Darwin had given to the world the law of evolution for the lower animals, so Marx had given to society the law of Dialectical Materialism.

Now a description of the philosophy of Communism which today holds 37 out of every 100 people in the world under its sway:

Lenin, who made Russia Communistic, once said that Communism combined the thought of Germany, France, and England. That was a very good description of it because Marx actually did get his philosophy from Germany, his sociology from France, and his economics from England.

To explain the philosophy of Communism, one would have to show how Dialectical Idealism became Dialectical Materialism. This we will do in terms of marriage. Imagine a love affair between a prize fighter, whose name is Mr. Motion, and a young poetess by the name of Miss Dreamer. They are not too well-matched; all he thinks about is fighting someone else. His fists are up looking for opposition, as he goes about bouncing on his toes and shaking his head. Miss Dreamer has no interest at all in his fighting. All she thinks about is rhyme, meter, and verse. She does not know how to make a pie. She could not sweep a floor. Despite the fact that it was a queer combination, they did get married, and Miss Dreamer thus became Mrs. Motion.

After a while, there appears on the scene a Mr. Trouble-maker, who introduces Mr. Motion to a girl whose name is Miss Mud. Miss Mud worked in a beauty parlor. All Miss Mud ever thought about was mud packs. When she was a girl, she used to make mud pies, and now that she was grown up, her greatest contentment in life was to plaster someone's face with mud. The story ends by the prize fighter leaving the dreamer and marrying Miss Mud. From that time on Miss Dreamer disappears and one sees only Mud and Motion.

This parable we now translate in terms of philosophy. Karl Marx went to the University of Berlin, where he was obliged to study the philosophy of Hegel. Hegel's philosophy was known as "Dialectical Idealism." Marx wrote his thesis on it, and, incidentally, he dedicated it with considerable foresight to his future father-in-law.

The philosophy of Hegel was first of all "Idealism"; it was concerned with thoughts, ideas, concepts, abstractions. "Dialectical" means Hegel's description of how thought grows, namely, by contradiction, by opposition, and by contrariety. Suppose the problem is how to decorate a room. Some suggest blue; others oppose it and recommend yellow. Out of this clash of ideas there finally is a decision to do it in yellow. Hegel would turn over in his grave if he ever heard dialectics explained that way. Though it is not adequate, it does convey, however, how opposition and negation do sometimes develop thought.

Hegel's basic idea was that all thought grows by contradiction. This is false, but we must let it pass to see how one false idea gives rise to another. Marx wrote his doctoral thesis on the philosophy of Hegel, using two early Greek thinkers to illustrate it. His thesis was so dialectical that he made the second sentence contradict the first and the third sentence reconcile as far as possible the first two.

Coming back to our analogy, Mr. Motion stands for the Dialectical in the thinking of Hegel, and Miss Dreamer stands for the Idealism. The two never should have been united, but both lovers and philosophers can sometimes do crazy things.

The moment arrives for Mr. Troublemaker to begin to do his work and to induce Motion and Dreamer to separate. Mr. Troublemaker is Karl Marx. The idea that the two ought to be divorced came in 1841, when Marx read a work of Feuerbach called *The Essence of Christianity*, which was an attack on the Idealism of Hegel. Feuerbach argued, "There is no mind, there is no thought, there is no spirit, no God—there is only matter. Man is what he eats." The former Miss Dreamer is about to be thrown out of the house. But some mate must be found for Mr. Motion.

Marx now got what he thought was a brilliant idea: Would it not be wonderful to take the dialectic which Hegel applied to ideas and apply it to matter? If you did, then you would have Dialectical Materialism—or matter in motion. In other words, Marx said: You don't need God to explain matter; matter is endowed with its own motion. Inside of everything is contradiction, opposition, contrariety, and out of that come the world, history, and society.

This is the philosophy of Communism. Marx now marries off the prize fighter, Mr. Motion, who stands for dialectics, to Miss Mud, who stands for matter, and out of this union was spawned the first child, called Soviet Russia. In more abstract terms, *reality is revolutionary;* its essence is conflict, internal tension, opposition.

It now remains to see how this was applied to the social order. The philosophy of Communism was made in Germany;

now it falls to France to help Marx formulate its application to society.

Marx visited in Paris a sociologist by the name of Proudhon, to whom he talked through an interpreter who later became one of Marx' enemies, the Russian Bukanin. Marx tried to sell the practical Frenchman on the idea of Dialectical Materialism. Night after night in a dull Teutonic fashion, he unfolded to Proudhon the weird thought that all matter is endowed with motion because it is full of contradictions. Proudhon answered, "Listen, Marx, you are a typical German philosopher—way up in the air. The universe is not full of contradictions; furthermore the big problem of the world is not how to marry off Hegel and Feuerbach so as to have Dialectical Materialism. The big problem in the world today is the problem of property." Proudhon had written a work on property. Proudhon explained to Marx, "I can see there is some contrast now and then between capital or those who own property, and labor or those who work with capital. But these two are not opposed one to the other as contradictions. They are both essential for the well-being of society." And he said to Marx, "I do not see how in Heaven's name you are ever going to apply your dialectics to these two elements."

But Marx was determined to keep the dialectic he got from Hegel. When he left the garret of Proudhon that night, he fancied that maybe he could put contradiction into society as he had put it in matter. This contradiction he determined to find between those who own property and those who do not. His conclusion was, "Just as I have shown that all matter is revolutionary, so now I will show that all society is revolutionary. The history of the world is nothing but the struggle between two classes—capital and labor, and out of the struggle comes a classless society, or 'Communism.' "

History must be rewritten to find that war and peace, progress and decay, are all explained in terms of class hate. There is no place for such human virtues as compassion or pity; society is *determined* to move on in a relentless struggle, until Communism takes over the world. Marx, of course, did not *explain* why, if everything is *determined*, revolutionists had to help bring it into existence, and why the process should stop with Communism. Why should not Communism beget its contrary, and then pass on to a higher synthesis?

His next idea was to explain that the nature of man is being destroyed in two ways: by private property and by religion. By private property, because man is subordinated to an employer; by religion, because man is subordinated to God. The conclusion was: "We can create a new man if we confiscate all property and if we persecute religion." In other words, confiscation and atheism are intrinsically united in Communism. As Marx wrote, "Communism begins where atheism begins." The economics of Communism was developed in England, but that we pass over for want of time.

Communism destroys human freedom. Man is free, thanks to two guarantees: one economic, the other spiritual. The economic guarantee of freedom is private property, for it enables man to call something his own which is *outside* himself. The spiritual guarantee of freedom is his soul, which

makes him independent of an earthly tyrant or a political dictator. Thanks to religion, his soul is his own on the *inside*, as
his property is his own on the outside.

If Communism is to enslave man and destroy his freedom,
it can do so only by wiping out man's two guarantees of freedom. This is done by destroying private property on the one
hand, and by atheism or the persecution of religion on the
other hand. These are the two fundamental concepts of Communism, and he who thinks it is an economic or political system
is ignorant of its nature.

Once, too, Dialectical Materialism is understood, one can
understand the attitude of the Soviets at the U.N. and at peace
conferences throughout the world. Their basic principle is
that the Communist revolution can come into being only by
creating contradiction, opposition, conflict, civil war and chaos
in society. Hence they must do everything to create confusion, obfuscation: one moment seeming like angels, the next
moment being like devils. If our Western politicians knew
something about Dialectical Materialism and the way it works
itself out at the peace tables, they would not be fooled by the
tactics of the Communists. They would know that the Soviets
cannot promote peace; they must work for disorder. How
long would doctors tolerate in their medical societies a small
group who believed that the only way to restore public health
was to inoculate everyone with leprosy?

Finally it must be remembered that the philosophy of Communism is not Russian in origin; it is Western. It belongs to
Western civilization. This is a horrible thought—the more

horrible because it is true. Communist philosophy is nothing but a hodgepodge, a potpourri, a mélange, a mixture of all of the cheap, deistic, skeptical, rationalistic, atheistic thinking of the eighteenth and nineteenth centuries. It is both a product and a judgment of the Western world: a product, because spawned by bad Western thinking; a judgment, because it now comes back to haunt us with its evil.

The conflict between the philosophy of Communism and the philosophy of a Christian civilization will not be settled by war. Nor will the Communist challenge be met by Western civilization trying to preserve the fruits of Christianity without its roots. The real solution of the conflict is the conversion of Russia and the return of Western people to the practical service of God which made them great. In other words, it is our hope that, in the recovery of God, the contest between Russia and the Western world will end in a tie, as we both accept Him, Our Way, Our Truth, and Our Life.

CHAPTER EIGHTEEN

Education

Much fun has been poked at education. Will Rogers once described "college-bred" as a "four-year loaf." A humorist of the last century affirmed that "being a widow for two years is far better than a college education." Robert Hutchins explained, "The reason we give sheepskins to college graduates is in order to cover up their intellectual nakedness." Another cautioned, "You can lead a boy to college, but you cannot make him think."

Despite these extreme views, every adult regrets that he did not study harder when in school. This is particularly true of Americans who visit France. They had a little book French in school, but they never seem to speak "book French" in Paris. Americans get angry because the horses and dogs understand French, and they do not. Then the American feels that the reason the French do not understand him is because the Frenchman is deaf, so he shouts. About the only one who understands an American in France is another American.

This discussion on education is not concerned so much with the vocational or professional side of it, but rather with the general philosophy of education governing colleges and universities.

The general aim of education is obviously to train the whole man—the intellect and the will, not just the mind alone. Knowledge is in the intellect or mind; character is in the will or our decisions. We would not buy a suit with one sleeve, nor a pair of pants with one leg. So, with education, it should not only perfect the mind but also build character. Education today gives little attention to the latter. But even in developing the intellect, education must understand its nature. To that one phase of the subject, this chapter is dedicated.

Education should maintain three goals in the training of the intellect:

1. Train it in the way of truth.
2. Correlate subjects with one another.
3. Emphasize depth, rather than froth.

1. *Truth*. The purpose of education is not primarily to train us for democracy, nor to enable us to make a living; the purpose of education is to give the mind truth, truth about everything: science, literature, history, art, philosophy, theology, etc.

We cannot serve democracy unless we recognize that we are persons and "have inalienable rights that come to us from God." We cannot make a living as an engineer unless we know the truths of engineering. But, beyond all these particular truths, the one basic truth that we have to learn is, of course, the truth of our own existence. We would not have a gadget in our house five minutes without knowing what it was for; yet some live twenty or sixty years without knowing why they are here or where they are going. When life is meaningless, it is dull; the absence of a goal or a purpose begets worries, anxieties, fears, psychoses, and neuroses. What is the use of living unless we know the purpose of living? The first knowledge that education should give us is: What is the truth about man? Why was he made? When all other temporal and proximate purposes have been attained or known, there still remains the ultimate purpose, namely, the attainment of perfect happiness, which is God.

Why is truth important? There is a theorem in psychology called "ideomotor," which means that every idea has a kind of motor power, or tends to work itself out into act. Suppose you are at a football game. You are in the stands where you can see the plays readily. From this superior position, you watch a fullback swing around right end; but you also see an opening around tackle. Your body moves instinctively in that direction. You had the idea in your mind, and the idea worked itself out into act. We cry when we hear bad news; we laugh when we hear a good joke.

Every idea that we have tends to some kind of expression. Our actions, therefore, can betray our ideas. It has been said that it makes no difference what you believe; it all depends upon how you act. This is nonsense, because we act upon our beliefs. As our food determines our health, so our ideas go into the making of our behavior.

Since every idea works itself out into act, it is important to put true ideas into our minds. The mind must be treated as gently as the stomach. We do not put garbage in the stomach. The government even "restricts our freedom" through food laws to protect our well-being. But our stomachs are not nearly as important as our minds. Some minds love to read murder stories in the press. A hatchet murder is thrilling! Some newspapers concentrate on news about murders, infidelities, adulteries, and slanders. All this filth gets into our heads and creates a tendency to work itself out into act.

It is true that Socrates contended, "Evil is ignorance." From this it has been argued that the way to make people virtuous is to educate them. But this is not true, not only because evil is more often made by the will or by our bad choices rather than by ignorance; but also because facts show that the best-educated are not always the most virtuous. Every D.D. ought to be a saint, but very few of them are. Education does not deliver us always from evil. Education conceivably could make clever devils instead of stupid ones; if we had to choose between the two, we would prefer the stupid devils.

From another point of view, when it is said that we ought to know evil, we must understand how evil is known. When Satan tempted our first parents in the Garden of Paradise, he argued, "God has forbidden you to eat of this tree of knowledge of good and evil. The reason He did so is this: God Himself knows the difference between good and evil. You do not. But if you did know the difference between good and evil, you would be like Him. He does not want you to be gods; this

is why He forebade you. Therefore, eat the fruit of the tree.
Know good and evil as He does, and 'you will be as gods.'"

The fallacy in Satan's argument was his failure to distin-
guish two ways of knowing anything. For example, typhoid
fever can be known as we know it now, negatively; we do
not have it. The evil is known by negation. There are some
people who know typhoid fever experimentally; they suffer
from it. How does God know evil? He knows evil negatively.
How do *we* know evil? We know evil as the typhoid fever
patient knows typhoid. It gets into us, it works its way not
only through the alleys and gateways of our body, but all
through our lives, until it eventually has the power to possess
us.

It is one thing to know intellectual errors, as the negation
of truth; it is quite another thing to know evil by infection.
The germ could ruin us. To know what dishonesty is one
need not be a thief. To know what "life" is, one need not be
an adulterer. Drunkenness can be known without being drunk.
Education which emphasizes the necessity of living evil in
order to know evil is in danger of making the mind captive
to evil. Values and joys are associated with temperance, which
the alcoholic does not know, and with innocence, which the
sex addict can never experience. Let a drunken man become
sober and he will see things as they are; let a skeptic turn to
the Diety and he will begin to know truth.

Our Blessed Lord associated truth with freedom, but not
evil. "The truth will make you free." Freedom alone does not
make truth; it does supply the condition of discovering it. But

the condition is not the cause. The real cause of freedom is truth. Only when we know the truth about an airplane are we free to pilot it; only when we know the truths of the science of medicine are we free to practice it; and only when we know the truth of life are we most free to live it.

2. *Correlation of studies.* Colleges offer hundreds of courses. A college catalogue we saw not very long ago had twenty-nine distinct courses on public speaking. There are not twenty-nine different things to say about public speaking. One thing certainly is: Do not read your manuscript or a teletype. I asked the Dean, "Why do you have twenty-nine courses?" His answer was, "Other universities do." They were "keeping up with the Joneses"!

In every college curriculum, some courses are more important than others. Here, we repeat, we are not speaking of vocational or professional training, but rather of general or liberal education. Courses should be arranged in a pyramid. The ancient Greeks illustrated the hierarchy of sciences by naming the three superior subjects of the mind.

The principle which guided them is still valid, namely, every superior subject illumines the lower one. If you pour water on top of a pyramid, it slowly seeps down on the ever-widening base. So the principles of metaphysics shed some light on mathematics; mathematics aids the knowledge of the universe; it also helps clarify music. In a musical composition, not every note has exactly the same stress; in language, not every word has the same emphasis; and in education, not every course has the same value.

Today the pyramid theory of education is replaced by the shelf theory. On a shelf are a number of bottles. The assumption is that when you go to college, it does not make any difference what course you take; you select any course that pleases your fancy. At the end of four years, you have collected sixty-four bottles, or sixty-four credits. It does not make a particle of difference what is in the bottles: sand, water, milk, Spanish, rug collecting, economics, or football coaching. They all have equal value. Bring them to the Dean and you get a sheepskin.

The result is that students are not getting the education they ought to receive; they get only a congeries of unrelated, disconnected, and disjointed subjects, which they and no one else can put together. An encyclopedia is not educated, despite its bursting knowledge, because it lacks the power to coordinate one subject with another. A truly educated man, on the contrary, sees a relationship between subjects, as he sees coordination in his own body and the universe. Any system of electives which ignores the unity of knowledge and the over-all purpose of life confuses the student rather than perfects him in truth.

Associated with the idea that no one subject is more important than another is the more false one that if you count something which has never been counted before, you are educated and really deserve a Ph.D. Hence the fondness for counting the vocatives, ablatives, and genitives in Virgil and the infinitives in Augustine. One university gave a Ph.D. degree for a thesis on "Four Ways of Cooking Ham." It almost makes one want to forget his philosophy! Another university gave a Ph.D. for a thesis on "Four Ways of Dishwashing." An M.A. degree was awarded for "A Psychological Study of the Post-rotational Eye Movement of the Squab." The prize for such theses goes to a Midwestern university, where a student finished his counting, but not his education, and received a Ph.D. for a dissertation on "The Microbic Content of Cotton Undershirts." How he must have scratched to get out that masterpiece!

3. *Depth.* Depth in education refers to deepening the knowledge of a subject, rather than treating one subject superficially and substituting another for it. Life unfolds through cell division; from one original cell there is multiplication until the complex organism with its faculties is built up. So with

knowledge. A truly educated person knows that in the nineteenth century the atom was considered to be homogeneous in structure, like a billiard ball. As knowledge deepened, it was found that at the center was a positive charge of electricity, and round about it were the negative charges, called neutrons. The atom was then revealed as a kind of miniature solar system. In the center was the proton, which corresponded to the sun; the neutrons were like the planets, Mercury, Venus, Jupiter, Mars, Saturn, earth, revolving round about it. As the mystery unfolded, Sir James Jeans said that the most scientific explanation of the atom is to be found in the Book of Genesis, where God said, "Let there be light." Now we know that the whole universe is intelligible in terms of light. There are two kinds of light: bottled light, or matter, and unbottled light, or illumination.

Only deepening knowledge is true education. But sometimes education rejects the clarification of mystery and goes in for *knowledge by substitution*. The automobile did not develop out of the horse and buggy; it was substituted for it. The electric light was not the unfolding of the light of a candle; it was a substitute for it. The mechanical view of substitution is applied to education to replace the biological view that truth is life and must be unfolded from the simple to the complex state. Students, instead of being given a very definite philosophy of life which they can explore all their days after they get their A.B. and their Ph.D., are given a point of view, a fad, a fancy, a theory which in ten or twenty years is antiquated. Forty years ago, a student, educated on the substitution theory, was told that the philosophy of Herbert Spencer was the last word in truth. Today, Spencer is forgotten. Freud will be forgotten in thirty years, as Spencer is forgotten now. Philosophies of life as changeable as a woman's hat are given

young minds, leaving them with no stable foundation on which they can build during life. It is positively amazing the amount of ignorance that can be accumulated in the form of useless facts and passing theories, sociological moods and philosophical fancies. A university that is materialistic in its thinking one decade, is idealistic in the next, another is Marxist one year, Fabian the next. The student who is given no fixed rule which he can explore all his life is made dizzy because the ground on which he stands is spinning. When the mind is without a fixed goal and a definite philosophy of life, from the constant tossing and spinning it becomes first confused, then bored, and finally despairing.

If, however, one has a philosophy of life that is solid and stands up against all vicissitudes, he can enter the labyrinth of life. He always carries with him a string into the dark places, and can always find his way back. But to lay down the tracks one year, and then tear them up the next year because one is not certain of his destination, is enough to drive the mind crazy.

In a democracy such as our own, we do not want *uniformity* of education; we want only a *unity* of education. Unity of education, in the sense that all will be good citizens dedicated to the preservation of the moral fabric of the nation and the continuation of its great traditions. But no uniformity of education, in the sense that everyone is to be poured into identically the same mold and measured by the same standards. To make all schools identical in a democracy is not to be democratic. Reduction of education to one type could be the beginning of the reduction of all minds to one party. Where there is uniform mass education it is easy for a dictator to take over; where there is diversity of points of view in the political, economic, and social order, there is a democracy under which men fall. There is uniformity of education in Russia; in America we want unity under which all men recognize themselves to be the possessors of rights and liberties as the "inalienable endowment of the Creator."

CHAPTER NINETEEN

Regressive Education

The New York Board of Education reported that during 1953 the younger generation broke 265,343 school windows. This averages about 72 a day, 3 an hour, or 1 every 20 minutes night and day. The Department of Justice announced at the same time that crime in the United States costs the American family $495 a year. A recent cartoon pictured some boys and girls in a classroom who had just tied the teacher to the desk and with axes in their hands were about ready to commit mayhem. Her feeble plea was, "Now, children, recess is over!"

Suppose we tried to concoct some theory of education which would produce juvenile delinquents and criminals. What would it be? Allowing our imagination to work, one might come up with a theory called "regressive education." Regressive education has three principles:

1. Man is an animal.
2. Youth must always be self-expressive.
3. There must never be any repression.

1. *Man is an animal.* The best way to make criminals in the next generation is to tell the children that they have no souls, no minds, no spirits; they are only animals with the same instincts, libidos, passions, emotions, drives, and urges. They perhaps are a little more complicated than an animal, but essentially they are beasts—"little beasts" it is true; but they will grow into "big beasts."

2. The second principle of regressive education, destined to produce criminals, is that we must always be *self-expressive* of these libidos and drives. One should talk as follows: "Down at the bottom of our brain is what is called an id; and over above it is a 'super-ego.' The id is the seat of passion and instinct which must always be given its release. The super-ego is religion and convention and morality, which repress individual expression. An animal never has complexes. Why not? Because it always follows its instincts. If man followed his instincts, he would never have them either. Express the id, which is the seat of the instinct; allow the sex instinct to assert itself. You will become abnormal if you allow the super-ego to thwart or stall your releases."

3. *No discipline.* Never correct a child when he is wrong, because if you tell a child he is wrong, he may develop a "guilt complex." This theory is called "regressive education" because by it man regresses to an animal. A brat has been defined as a smart boy who does not smart where he ought to smart. A brat is also a boy who always is on his pest behavior. We forgot to say that this theory came from the brain of the well-known professor, Letem B. Brats. Professor Letem B. Brats has no

children, but he has written a number of books on how to
bring up children. His greatest contribution to education is the
new idea that a child should never be corrected. Professor
Letem B. Brats has a dog. But he will not allow that dog to jump
up on the furniture; nor will he allow the dog to bring bones
into the house. He has even insisted that the dog be house-
broken, but the children he allows to run wild. It seems odd for

Professor Letem B. Brats to insist on disciplining a dog, but not
a child—but there it is!

Is there anything wrong with the theory of Professor
Letem B. Brats? His basic principle that man is an animal certainly can be questioned. If man is an animal, why is it that
man has complexes and an animal has none? Did you ever hear
of a rhinoceros going to a psychoanalyst? Did you ever hear
of a rooster with an inferiority complex? Did you ever hear
of a hog with an Electra complex? There is not an animal in

the world that has a psychosis or neurosis. Why does man have them and not beasts? Man can have a complex because he is complex, that is, made up of body and soul, flesh and spirit. In addition to his passions, libidos, instincts, and urges, he has a soul which is capable of knowing the Infinite and the Eternal. Only the Eternal can make a man despair. It is the desire for the Infinite in man which makes it possible for him to feel frustrated. It is the spirit in him that makes him different from the beast. It is true that everyone should live according to his nature. A hog uses its instincts according to hog nature. Man has not a hog nature, but a rational nature. Therefore, he will use his passions according to right reason and not according to impulse.

If I tried to open a beer bottle with a fountain pen, not only would I not open the beer bottle, but I would break the pen, because the purpose of the pen is to write and not open beer bottles. Man has a purpose, which is to achieve perfect Life, Truth, and Love; when he turns away from that destiny, he not only misses happiness on earth, he even hurts himself psychically.

Professor Letem B. Brats, in defense of his theory, once declared himself against morality, in favor of hygiene. "If you tell them the danger of certain practices, they will never resort to those practices." He gives the example of smallpox in the house. "If you saw a smallpox sign on the house, you would not go into the house, would you?"

It sounds very good, but Professor Letem B. Brats forgets

that there is no man in the world who has an impulse or a drive
to break down the door of a smallpox room, but many humans
have passions and urges to break down other kinds of doors.
Those inordinate instincts have to be repressed, not because
they may produce an unhealthy condition, but because they
are just plain wrong.

The second principle of self-expression is not always right.
Professor Letem B. Brats assumes that every psychological
complex is cured by a physiological outlet. Curing a bad heart
by bloodletting is not a recommended practice in medicine.
Certainly those who have a psychic urge to do harm to others
should not be given a machine gun. If repression is always
wrong, why is it that political anarchy and carnal license are
combined phenomena of troubled times?

Self-expression is not always right. Suppose that a soldier
is on duty in the front lines. But at a critical moment in battle
he has an urge to leave his post. As he runs away from the lines,
should the captain say to him, "Young man, I want to con-
gratulate you. Too long have soldiers been following these
mid-Victorian taboos of being loyal to their country and
staying at their posts in the midst of danger. I recommend
you for the Congressional Medal of Honor. You are self-
expressive."

If a robber breaks into a bank and is caught as he emerges
with his loot by a policeman, should the banker be self-expressive and say, "What is wrong with robbery? After all, I take
an interest in other people's money—generally 6 per cent. He

takes 100 per cent interest in other people's money. I praise him for being more self-expressive than I am. Let him keep the money."

Some men, it is said, do have urges to do something to their mothers-in-law. Should they be self-expressive unto violence? Should the judge then quiz the son-in-law in such a manner as this: "Is it true that you killed your mother-in-law?" "Yes, I killed my mother-in-law." "How did you kill her?" "I killed her with a club." "What kind of club?" "A golf club." "I know, but which club?" "The niblick." "Well, if you were going to kill her, that was the club to use."

The third principle of Professor Letem B. Brats is never to scold, reprimand, spank, or even tell a child that he is wrong. But if repression is always wrong, why does not Professor Letem B. Brats condemn women for dieting? That is a repression of the hunger instinct. If it is right to repress eating for the sake of the appearance of the body, why should it not be right to repress certain evil urges for the sake of the soul? If repression is wrong, why are those who practice the most self-control the most normal, and why are libertines abnormal? It is not underprivileged persons, but the overprivileged, who are mentally sick.

When one thing is repressed something else is liberated. If evil is repressed, good emerges; if good is repressed, evil emerges. For example, a woman declares her husband to be "so devoted when he is sober." Evidently, then, devotedness expresses itself as alcoholism is repressed; and as alcoholism is expressed, devotedness is repressed. Repression, in the moral order, can be liberation.

Every college student in the United States who has had a good course in philosophy knows this principle: *Quidquid recipitur, secundum modum recipientis recipitur*—"Whatever is received is received according to the manner of the one receiving it."

Pour water into the red glass, and it looks red; pour it into a green glass, and it looks green; pour it into a black glass, it will look black. When you pour truth into mind *A* and pour it into mind *B*, it does not have the same effect, though it is identically the same truth. *A* may accept it, and *B* may not. The difference is not in the truth; rather the difference is in the mental soil upon which the seed of truth falls. It is not ignorance alone that is the cause of unbelief. Another and more important cause is behavior.

If a number of men were placed at different heights, one would declare that the sun had risen, another that it was rising, and the third that it had not risen. We should ascribe the diversity not to anything in the sun, but to the different attitudes of the observers. The attitude people take toward truth depends upon the moral attitude of those hearing it. A French infidel once said to Pascal, "If I had your principles, I would be a better man." Pascal said, "Begin with being a better man, and you will soon have my principles." If we do not live as we think, we soon begin to think as we live; we make a philosophy to suit our bad behavior. As Aristotle said, "Wickedness corrupts a man's nature, gives him false principles and evil measures of things." A covetous man understands nothing to be good that is not profitable. It is hard for a man to admit a reason against the thing he loves. Men often question truth because they hate it in practice. If they changed their lives, they would change their thinking. Skepticism is not an intellectual position, but a moral position; it results from living outside of the order of God.

Man is not just a spectator of reality. The world and the social order are not something that we watch indifferently, as we watch a drama seated in the theater. If we are to build citizens for America, we must educate our youths to the realization of the greater truth—that they are not only spectators of reality, but also creators. This power of creativity comes from the fact that every one of us is endowed with a soul, with choice and deliberation. To each and every one has been given the alternative of saying "aye" or "nay" to the great God Who made us. We are creators of our destiny. If anyone says, "Well, if God knew I would be a wicked man, why did He make me?" The answer is that God did not make you wicked—you made yourself. This is a world of soul making, and the truest form of self-expression is the salvation of one's soul.

CHAPTER TWENTY

Women Who Do Not Fail

The level of any civilization is the level of its womanhood. The reason is to be found in the difference between knowing and loving. When we know something, we bring it *down* to the level of our intelligence. Examples of abstract subjects must be given to children to suit the level of their minds. But when we love something, we always have to go *up* to meet it. For example, if we want to master music, we must obey its laws and meet its demands. If we love a foreign language enough to study it, we must accept its grammar, its spelling, and its word meanings. Since a woman is loved, it follows that the nobler a woman is, the nobler man will have to be to be deserving of that love. That is why the level of any civilization is always the level of its womanhood.

There are three types of women who keep civilization at a high level.

First are women who do not fail in the social, political, and economic order. One immediately meets an objection: Does professional life harden a woman? It is sometimes asserted that it does, but this comes from a misunderstanding. Sometimes women in professional life do become hard, but this is due to other factors. A woman becomes hard only when she loses or surrenders an opportunity to manifest those specifically feminine qualities of sympathy, kindness, and tenderness.

Every woman in the world was made to be a mother, either physically or spiritually. To limit the discussion to professional women, we here ignore physical motherhood and limit ourselves to spiritual motherhood. A woman in professional life is happy when she has an occasion to be feminine. A man is the guardian of nature, but a woman is the custodian of life. The exercise of this protective, creative, uplifting vocation is the source of her power. She cannot look at a limping dog, she cannot see a flower with a broken stem, without her heart, her mind, and her hands going out to these things, as if to bear witness that she was appointed by God as the guardian and custodian of life. These emotional needs cannot be disregarded without defeminizing her.

The woman who does not fail in professional life is the woman, therefore, who manifests this feminine quality of "equity." There is a world of difference between law and equity. Law is concerned with rules, exactness, justice. There is an inexorable quality about it. Equity is concerned with the circumstances that escape law, with extenuating circumstances, and personal excuses; it always finds some reason for not being too strict and too rigorous.

Henry Adams, in his *Mont-Saint-Michel and Chartres*, tells the story of the Cathedral of Chartres. He pictures on opposite sides of this great cathedral magnificent windows given by the

rival families of Pierre de Dreux and Blanche of Castile. They seem to be carrying on a civil war across the bulk of that cathedral. But the author reflects that high on the main altar stood the statue of Our Lady of Equity, listening, as it were, to the disputes, and adjudicating them with mercy, kindness, and tenderness.

If a woman does not have an opportunity in her working hours, between nine and five, to manifest those feminine qualities of tenderness, meekness, and gentleness, then she will have to find occasion after those hours if she is to keep normal. Woman, by vocation, is called to temper the world of justice with love, and to present the extenuating circumstances that fall outside the rigors of law. The feminine by nature is linked to clemency and thus prevents man from being conquered in advance through despair. In the family, as the mother is the intercessor of mercy for the child in the face of the justice of the father, so in society she is synonymous with equity, forgiveness, and love. In manifesting these qualities, even in the professional world, she is a woman who does not fail.

The second type of woman who does not fail is the one who manifests physical motherhood. Every mother is the bearer of God's gifts to man. She adds a new dimension to her love of husband. A man is afraid of dying; a woman is afraid of not living. A woman marries to have children; she thinks in terms of perpetuation. A man marries to have a woman. The image of man as a rational creature made by God has been deformed by Marx, Freud, and others. It is woman's role to restore that image by giving the human race a fresh start.

After motherhood, comes mothercraft, or the teaching of obedience to children. Obedience is the condition of wisdom, as scientists so clearly reveal. A scientist, if he is ever to know nature, has to sit passively before it. He says to nature, "Here I am sitting before you. You teach me. I will learn from you." To the extent that he is obedient to nature, he is wise about its laws. When finally he has the laws of nature in his own mind, then he can convert them into technical power and the progress of civilization.

And so it is with a child. When a child is obedient, he learns wisdom. The more we obey the laws of anything, the more they reveal their secrets to us. "If any man will do My Will, he will know My doctrine." The obedient child who has learned moral wisdom from its parents is prepared to use that wisdom later on for his own perfection. No one can ever command who has not first learned to obey. If parents surrender responsibility to their children, the state will take up the slack. State power is the effect of the breakdown of family authority. Mothers, more than politicians, are the preservers of freedom and democracy.

Youth grows to maturity like wheat in a field. Wheat is healthy when rooted in the soil and in communion with the sky. Youth is normal when rooted in the family and in communion with the invisible forces that make the soul. Take the grain of wheat out of that field before it is ripe, and it acquires a false independence which withers it to death. When a child is up-rooted from the wisdom and obedience of a home, he is like that grain of wheat that has been pulled up unripe; he begins to acquire an importance which actually he does not have, be-cause he is not yet mature. This may explain the present mood to have youth talk on all subjects before they have learned them. Certain types of delicate flowers can be killed by being transplanted to new soil too quickly.

The third type of womanhood which does not fail civiliza-tion is that which seeks to preserve ideals of purity and good by the consecration of virginal lives to God. Virginity is not opposed to love, as wealth is opposed to poverty. Virginity is the mountain-peak of love. When spoiled lovers seek to make a false infinite out of a succession of finite loves, it is helpful to civilization to know there are some whose first love is their last love, and their last love is the love of God.

Who does the most to preserve patriotism in a nation? It is not the politicians who talk about duties; it is not the dramatist who glorifies its past. The ideals of patriotism in a nation are best preserved by soldiers on the battlefield who are prepared to die, if need be, to prove that other values are unimportant compared with the great love of country.

Why should there not be women who will do for love what soldiers do for patriotism? Should there not be some women who will love God so deeply and so profoundly that they will sacrifice all lesser loves in order to preserve, for a weak and sinful and possibly sex-minded world, the real understanding of love? They keep love pure. Everyone can readily understand why a young woman should love a human heart for a life span, but some find it hard to understand why anyone should love the Divine Heart. But if the spark gives joy, why should not the Flame, which is God?

A rose in a garden has its own father, its own mother, its own hopes and aspirations for the future; when there is rain, it has its own tears; when there is sunshine, it has its own smile. Out into the garden there comes a hand, plucks up the rose, and destroys it, as far as the rose's environment is concerned. But no injustice is done, for the hand of man is above the rose, and he may use it for his own purposes.

In a human family is a human rose, with her own real father and mother, brothers and sisters, hopes and aspirations for the future, her own real laughter, her own real tears. From High Heaven there comes the Hand of the Heavenly Gardener, Who reaches down, plucks her up, and "destroys" her life as far as human environment is concerned; but there is no injustice done, because, as the hand of man is above the rose, so the Hand of God is above the soul, and He may solicit it for His own nobler purposes.

But it may be asked, What favors and blessings accrue to the rose that is plucked? This rose that is plucked is touched by the human hand and even pressed to human lips. Its rose life is shortened, but what a beautiful life it now begins to lead with man! In like manner, the young human life which is called in vocation is put into the vase of consecrated service of God, while the refreshing waters of sanctifying grace touch it from day to day. Its human life is shortened, yes, but what a beautiful life it begins to lead with God! This is the love Francis Thompson calls the "passionless passion, and wild tranquillity." These are the women who do not fail.

In the great crises of Our Lord on Good Friday, there were many instances of men failing; but there is not a single instance of a woman failing. Peter denied Him, Judas blistered His lips with a kiss; the Apostles slept. But women solaced Him on the way to Calvary; a woman made her way into Pilate's courtroom to plead His case. A woman wiped His face on the road to Calvary and became known as "Veronica," which means the "true image," for He left the imprint of His Sacred Face on her veil.

At the foot of the Cross there were three women, and their names were Mary—Mary Magdalene, Mary of Cleophas, and Mary of Nazareth, the Mother of the Saviour. These three women symbolized the three women who do not fail civilization. Mary Magdalene symbolizes those who take hold of tangled skeins of a wrecked and ruined life and weave out of them the beautiful tapestry of saintliness and holiness; she is the model of women who inspire others in the social, political, and economic order to make love redemptive through kindness, affection, and sacrifice.

Mary of Cleophas, the mother of James the Less, taught obedience to her son—an obedience that eventually made him the apostle of the Wisdom of the World. She is the model of all others who raise children in virtue and goodness.

Finally, there was Mary the Contemplative, who left the lights and glamour of the world for the shade and shadows of the Cross, where saints are made.

These are the women who do not fail. We salute them! We toast them—not as modern women, "once our superiors, now our equals." Rather, we toast them as women who never fail, women who were closest to the Cross on Good Friday, and first at the tomb on Easter Morn.

CHAPTER TWENTY-ONE

Social Problem

A lawyer, anxious to justify himself, once asked Our Lord,
"Who is my neighbor?" The reason he sought to justify himself was that he knew he did not possess that Eternal Life of
which Our Lord spoke. Wanting an excuse for not having it,
he asked the question. He wanted declared beforehand the
extent of his obligations. Peter has asked about the limits of
forgiving; the lawyer now inquires the limits of giving. Is it
one of my race, my nation, my class, or one of my friends?
And to what degree am I bound to assist? The Saviour answered by telling the story of the Good Samaritan. The point
of the parable is not "Who is my neighbor?" but "Have you
the neighborly spirit?" Instead of asking, "Is this a worthy
object of charity?" Our Blessed Lord, suggesting ourselves,
asks, "Are we a worthy subject for charity?"

That parable of the Good Samaritan centers about a man
who went down from Jerusalem to Jericho. One goes *down*
from Jerusalem to Jericho. In that distance of about twenty-
four miles, there is a descent of three thousand feet, Jericho
being six hundred feet below the level of the Mediterranean.

There is only one part in that road where there suitably could be an inn, for there is only one place where there is water and a plateau. Everywhere along that road—it is still called the "Bloody Road"—it is possible for robbers to hide.

Some years ago, going down that road, I stopped at an Arab's hut and tiny restaurant and asked the owner if he had ever heard the story of the Good Samaritan. He said that he had not. I told him, "You are losing good business; everybody knows the story of the Good Samaritan." I asked him for a bucket of paint and with red paint I painted the sign, "The Good Samaritan Inn."

The traveler who went down from Jerusalem to Jericho was attacked by robbers, left wounded and half dead. A priest and a Levite passed by the wounded man, but a Samaritan, a member of a despised race, put the man on his beast, brought him to the inn, poured oil and wine in his wounds, gave the innkeeper two days' wages, and asked the innkeeper to care for him, saying, "I will come back again and pay you what I owe, over and above what I have given you.

The Good Samaritan was the one who had compassion for the wounded man. Our Lord then asked the lawyer, "Which of these three, in your opinion, was a neighbor to him that fell among robbers?" He answered, "He that showed mercy to him." The lawyer did not say the Samaritan, because his national prejudices forbade him to pronounce the name. The Lord answered, "Go, and do thou in like manner."

Modernizing the parable, we find four problems of social work:

1. Who create social problems?
2. Who ignore social problems?
3. The professional solution of those who work out of duty.
4. The real solution of those who work out of love.

Who create social problems? In the parable, the problem was created by an act of violence on the part of the robbers. The origin of social problems today is no different. The violence of World War II created 63 million refugees, many of whom threw themselves upon the earth as something more friendly than the hearts of men. Refugees are constantly pouring out of those lands where the violence of Communism is rampant. Nobody is a refugee going back into Communist slavery, not even the American Communists found guilty under the law. When offered the choice of going to Russia or to jail, they always say, "I will take an American jail, but I will not go back to Russia."

Social problems arise also from exploitation, for example, when capitalism treats the worker as a "hand," and when labor calls an unnecessary strike which paralyzes the common good. Educators are also guilty of violence when they tell students that they have no intellect, no free soul, but are beasts and act like beasts. To be a victim of intellectual robbers who despoil man of his Divine image is to create the gravest of social problems.

Who ignore the social problem? The social problem is ignored, obviously, by the Communists. The Communist philosophy as given by Marx is this: A person of and by himself is without any value. Unless an individual belongs to the revolutionary class, he is without worth. Communism then liquidates millions of persons for which it cares nothing, so long as the Communistic core or species continues to exist. Such are those today who boast of their love of the poor, who pass by the wounded people of the earth. They are the heirs of the priest and the Levite who passed by the traveler to Jericho. One often wonders what they did after they passed by that wounded man. I think they went either to Jerusalem or to Jericho and reported the matter to organized charity—after first filling out five long forms.

Others who ignore the social problem—and thank God, they are only a minority—are those in the field of social work who, influenced by the Marxist or Communist philosophy, believe that there are only social problems, but no personal problems. They assume that you can manipulate society as you manipulate machinery; and once you understand social laws thoroughly, then all individual problems will be solved. The masses alone matter; a person is not to be seen except in relation to his social utility. Mankind is studied like nature; it is always a social study, never a study of individuals, each with inalienable rights and an actual or potential child of God.

The error in this thinking is to forget that society is basically made up only of persons. Human nature is not to be studied like physical nature. One can be objective in studying stars, crayfish, and atoms. But human emotions, passions, prejudices, love, and hate are involved in personal relations. It is a fallacy to believe, therefore, that we can study human society as one studies ants or porpoises, though both travel in groups.

It is well to make an investigation of a problem before attempting a solution, but when the investigation is made more important than the problem to be solved, then there is "confusion worse confounded." A growing tendency is prevalent among charitable or educational foundations to spend greater fortunes making investigations than in helping human beings directly. It is well to make investigations when the alternatives are unknown. For example, if one wanted to find out which the American people like better, a singing commercial or a spoken commercial, a statistical study would be necessary. But when people are hungry and unclothed, one does not make an investigation; one first feeds, clothes, and cares for them, and then one counts them. That was what Our Blessed

Lord did when He found the multitude in the desert. He said, "They were a sheep without a shepherd," and so He fed them all. It was in feeding them that it was discovered there were five thousand.

A picture magazine once carried a series of photographs of a person prostrate on the subway steps of New York. This individual was wounded, had fainted, or had had a heart attack. A photographer stood there for an hour, taking pictures of everyone passing by this stricken man. The pictures appeared in this magazine in order to indicate that no one was interested in the individual. Why did not the photographer help? There must also have been a number of people who, when they saw the photographer taking pictures, thought the incident might be a fraud. There are more subtle ways in our generation of passing by human wrecks than the apparently cold way of the priest and Levite. If the stricken man had been of their race, they would have helped. The danger today is in believing there are no sick people, there is only a sick society; that toothaches are not personal worries, but only dental problems to be treated en masse.

Professional workers. By the professional worker is not here meant the organized social worker. The professional worker is here understood as one who, like the innkeeper, receives a wage for doing social work; but he works out of duty, just as the innkeeper received two days' pay. It was necessary for the loving hand of the Samaritan to come back to aid the professional worker.

Professional workers are not necessarily in nonreligious organizations. Many a trained social worker is in a purely secular organization but is, nevertheless, working out of love and, therefore, belongs in the category of those who really solve social problems. It is even possible that there could be some social workers in religious organizations who are working out of duty, but not out of love. Despite all the good that the duty workers do, it is not yet the real solution of the problem of charity, for the simple reason that they always work within limits. They believe in moderation. They believe one can go "too far" in human kindness. "We close at five." "You say that the family has not had food in twenty-four hours and you have no coal? Well, sorry, this is Washington's Birthday. Call us on Monday, and we will handle your case." A limit of service is reached, because duty is the motive. This is not to minimize the role of duty workers amidst human beings; it is only a question of pointing out the difference between duty and love.

A democracy must not throw all the burden of social problems upon professional workers and professional organizations. Suppose the owner of an automobile gave the right to drive the automobile to the governor, the right to fill the tires with hot air to the ward leader, the right to buy gas to the lieutenant governor. It would not be long before the owner would no longer be free to drive his automobile. As American people surrender their responsibility to the poor, sick, and aged in the community, they also surrender their freedom. The best preservative of freedom in any democracy is a recognition that we all have personal responsibility to the unhealthy and anemic members of our society. Socialism increases in direct ratio and proportion with the surrender of personal responsibility to neighbor.

The real solution is the solution of love. The Good Samaritan showed "compassion." Sympathy of the weak for the strong is natural, for thus do the weak acquire strength and the hungry receive food. But sympathy of the strong for the weak is not so natural, because it means an apparent loss of strength, resources, or time to those who can give nothing in return.

Those who work for love proceed on the principle that the rich need the poor more than the poor need the rich. By rich is meant those who have relatively more than those who are in grave need. The poor need the rich in order that they may have a roof over their heads, food in their stomachs, clothes on their backs, shoes on their feet. The rich need the poor in order that they may justify their stewardship of wealth, that they may thank God for the blessings that they have received, that they may have His grace in their hearts and His blessing on their being. The poor need the rich only for material reasons, but the rich need the poor for spiritual reasons. Hence, Our Blessed Lord said that those who have money are to use their money to make friends with it. Give it to the poor and they will intercede for us on the last day. As a beggar once said to someone at a church, "If you do not help me, who will intercede for you on the last day?"

Then, those who love for a Divine reason also have a different way of handling the poor from anyone else. The difference between charity and philanthropy can be illustrated

by a house. On the second floor live those with some super-
fluities; on the first floor live those who lack necessities. Philanthropy will leave the second floor and go down to the poor to
supply their needs. But after it has done that, it returns to the
comfort and maybe luxuries of its own floor. This is com-
mendable and necessary, but it is not perfect love. St. Paul
said that if he distributed all his goods to the poor, and lacked
charity or love of God, it would profit him nothing for eternal
salvation. In true Divine love, those who have passed over to
those who have not, never again come back. They stay there
until the needy have been relieved of their sorrow, their pain,
or their poverty, just as the model and inspiration, Our Blessed
Lord, came down to this earth, crossed from the line of innocence over to the line of sinners, stayed with them, suffered
with them, until He finally redeemed them. Saints understand
this best. Each one says in his heart, "While there is pain, I
suffer; while there is need, I want; while there is crime, I am
guilty."

Those who love know that everything must be done for
a Divine motive; even the drink of cold water must be given
in His Name. On the last day, even the great lovers of the
poor will be surprised. To those on His right hand, He will
say:

For I was hungry, and you gave me food,
    Thirsty, and you gave me drink;
I was a stranger, and you brought me home,
    Naked, and you clothed me,
Sick, and you cared for me, a prisoner, and you came to me.

The great lovers of the poor who did things in His Name will be surprised that He was so pleased; they will wonder when they served Him. The nurse will ask, "You mean when I took care of the patient in Room 238, I took care of You?" "You mean file number 164 of our social organization was You?" And the Saviour will answer:

> Believe Me, when you did it to one of the least
> Of My brethren here, you did it to Me.

When people die, their friends ask, "How much did they leave?" But the angels of Heaven ask, "How much did they take with them?"

CHAPTER TWENTY-TWO

Suffering

The subject of suffering may be discussed under the following heads:

1. The paradoxes of suffering.
2. Two ways of meeting pain or suffering.
3. How to accept it.

The paradoxes. Contemporary civilization is a strange mixture of material prosperity and, at the same time, a tremendous amount of inner and mental discontent. The per capita income of the United States is about $1,750. But there is also tremendous inner unhappiness. Fifty-one per cent of the hospital beds of the United States are occupied by mental patients. The wearied minds do not multiply because of prosperity, though it is true that abundance alone does not make happiness. Inner joy, it is too little understood, is associated not with *having*, but with *being*. The rich are becoming bored, as the tragic sense of life increases. This inner discontent and unhappiness caused by man's trying to put the infinite into the finite. Our souls were made to hold the ocean of perfection, so they quickly become weary when we settle only for a cupful of the ocean of life. As we get closer to the fire, we feel a greater heat; as we get closer to the Infinite for which we are made, our joy increases. Obviously settling for some kind of temporal security does not completely satisfy the soul. As Franz Werfel said, "This line of the finite must be crossed somehow or other. It is crossed above by faith; it is crossed below by insanity."

The second paradox is that we have a greater capacity for pain than we have for pleasure. A pleasure can reach a point where it will give us pain, for example, tickling. Pleasures also need a greater stimulus to produce an equal reaction. The curve of pleasure rises quickly, but when had too often, it drops suddenly. Honeymoons do not last long. In anticipation, a pleasure can often be greater than in the realization. In dreams, pleasure comes on a silver platter, but the actual meal is unsatisfying.

Suffering, on the contrary, increases, and our capacity for it often increases. We go to a dentist and we feel that if he drills five minutes more and goes six feet deeper, we just could not stand it. We stand it all right! And then he continues to bore until we fear he is going to hit oil. We still stand it! Many in sickbeds have felt that they exhausted themselves months or years ago, but they still can go on suffering.

Why do we have a greater capacity for pain than for pleasure? Probably because it was intended by God that all pain should end on this earth. The capacity for it is great in order that it may be exhausted here, for there is another life where tears will be wiped away: "the sorrows of this life are not worthy to be compared with the joys that are to come." But pleasure and happiness are not intended to be exhausted here; that comes elsewhere, being reserved for Heaven.

Double reaction to pain. Robert Louis Stevenson wrote:

> Two men looked out through prison bars.
> One saw mud; the other stars.

One reaction to pain can be rebellion; the other can be resignation. Those who rebel against it see no purpose in pain; but those who see it in relation to saving the soul, turn it into what is creative. When the universe is opaque and nothing is seen beyond, suffering is devoid of meaning. The universe is as transparent as a windowpane to those who see that "all things cooperate unto God in those who are called to be saints."

These two attitudes toward pain were perfectly exemplified by the two thieves and revolutionists crucified on either side of Our Divine Lord. Both of them suffered exactly the same torture. When they felt the impress of the nail on their hands, they blasphemed. Then they heard the First Word spoken by the One on the central cross. It was an unusual word He spoke. Generally, when men are sentenced to die, they protest their innocence, or condemn those who condemn them, or else ask for forgiveness. But here, for the first time in the history of the world, the Son of God on the Cross was saying, "Father, forgive them for they know not what they do."

When the thief on the left heard this cry, he asked Our Lord to prove His Power by stepping down from the Cross and by taking him down. That to him was a sign of Omnipotence—to stop that pain and suffering. Power, to that thief on the left, was to be used, not to make him better, but to enable him to go on with the dirty business of thieving. He could not assimilate pain; it came to him like foreign substance to the stomach that could not digest it. The result was that it intensified his rebellion to a point where his mouth became a crater of hate and a volcano of blasphemy. No one is better for pain; he could conceivably be worse. Unspiritualized suffering degenerates the soul. Refusing to think of pain as related to anything else intensifies the thought of self and thereby deepens egotism.

But the thief on the right, when he heard that prayer for forgiveness, began to see a relationship between his sufferings and his guilt. Some sparks from the central cross ignited some inflammable material in his soul, and in the belfry of his conscience the bell began to toll. He spoke to his brother thief, and he said, "Fear ye not? We suffer the just reward of our crimes, but this Man has done no wrong." Then turning to the Divine Saviour, he prayed, "Remember me when Thou shalt come into Thy Kingdom." Kingdom? Did He Who apparently was a fellow criminal have a Kingdom? The thief looked at the crown of thorns and saw there a royal diadem; the nail was to him as a scepter of power and authority; His crucifixion was His installation, and His blood, the royal purple. He asked only to be remembered. The response came back, "This day thou shalt be with Me in Paradise." "Thou"—it was the foundation of democracy; the worth of a single soul. "Thou shalt be with Me," I always wondered why He said "in Paradise"—to be with Him in Paradise! And the thief died a thief! For he stole Paradise; Paradise can be stolen again.

The use of pain. Pain can be used for *expiation* of our own failings and sins or in *reparation* for the failings and the sins of others.

Expiation. I was a boy about eight or nine years of age, and my brother and I were playing ball in the back yard. I threw a ball accidentally through the neighbor's window. Mother heard it, and she called us in. She sent us to our piggy bank and made us take some money out, go over to the man next door, pay him for the broken window, and also ask him to forgive us.

Now, why not merely ask for forgiveness for breaking the window? Many think that when they do anything wrong, all they have to do is ask to be forgiven. This is only half the story. Every act of injustice disturbs order. That disorder often has to be righted. For example, if I stole a watch, I might regret it and say to the person, "I am awfully sorry; I stole your watch. Will you forgive me?" He would say, "All right, I will forgive you," but he certainly would also say, "Give me back my watch." Returning the watch would prove the sincerity of my desire for forgiveness.

If we have sins—and who in the Name of God has not?— we can ask the Good Lord to take our pains in expiation and atonement. For illegitimate pleasures we make compensation by offering up the sufferings imposed on us, that our ledger on the last day will not find us in the red.

The second way suffering can be used is in *reparation*. Here we offer it up for others, not just for ourselves. In the physical order, doctors graft skin from a back to a face to restore burned tissue. If a person is suffering from anemia, doctors will transfuse blood from a healthy member of society to the anemic person in order to cure the person of that condition. If it is possible to transfuse blood, is it not possible to transfuse prayer? If it is possible to graft skin, is it not possible also to graft sacrifice and suffering? We live in a world in which we live on the work of others. We do not raise sheep, though we wear woolen clothes. Others do that work for us. So in the great spiritual community of the lovers of God it is possible to offer up pain and suffering in order that others who lack love of God may find it through our efforts. That is reparation.

If it be asked why we should offer our sufferings in expiation or reparation, the answer is because we love. Love does not kill pain, but love can diminish it. A mother sits up all night with her sick child. To the neighbors it is agony; to the mother it is love. There are many real lovers in the world who would willingly take on the pains and the agonies of others if they possibly could. Love in the face of sorrow does not seek isolation. It wants to take on that pain as its own. Why should not love in the face of sin and evil want to do the same thing? The great tragedy of our world is that most people who suffer have no one to love.

What is mysterious is not the suffering, but how much is missed when we do suffer! Think of all the feverish brows in hospitals who cannot sanctify that pain by correlating it to Our Lord with a crown of thorns. Think of the wounded who could sanctify their wounds if they only knew how, by correlating them in some way with Hands that were riven with nails. Think of all the aching hearts with worries, anxieties, and fears who could bear the cross if they only loved a Heart that was opened by a lance.

CHAPTER TWENTY-THREE

How Traitors Are Made

There are four steps in the making of a traitor:

1. Spiritual decay.
2. Social veneering.
3. Mask of patriotism.
4. Disillusionment and despair.

1. *Spiritual decay*. A man rots on the inside before he betrays on the outside; every act of outward treason is prefaced by some betrayal in the mind. He who has divorced himself from his country has already had one or two other divorces. One could be the divorce of his soul from God; the other could be the divorce of spouse from spouse. Given the first two, the divorce of man from his country follows as night the day. Any civilization in which a Mrs. Brown is willing to become a Mrs. White or a Mrs. White is willing to betray her professed lifelong loyalties to become a Mrs. Green will also be a civilization in which an American will soon be willing to call himself a Red. As Marx said, "Where atheism begins, Communism be-

gins." No man of practical, strong faith ever became a Communist. The exile of God in Communist society has necessarily entailed the tyrannization of man; the repudiation of God in the human soul is the prelude to the acceptance in an individual of the tyranny of Communism.

Every traitor has his father, and the patron of all traitors was Judas.

How this and the other stages of disloyalty are represented in his life will now be indicated. It is not to be thought that Judas betrayed because he was avaricious, for such was not the foundation of his treachery. The first record that we have of the break was after Our Blessed Lord had multiplied the loaves and the fishes and the crowd sought to crown Him a king. Our Blessed Lord, refusing earthly royalty, fled into the mountains alone. The next day when the crowd followed Him across the waters, He chided them for wanting earthly bread while reminding them that He was the Bread of Life. As the life of the body is the soul, so He promised to be the life of the soul of man as He called Himself the Living Bread descended from Heaven.

As soon as Judas heard it, his obvious reaction was, "This is too spiritual for me. Our Lord refused to become a king; now He is too much interested in the soul." The Gospel here records that Judas at that moment sought to betray Him. Though money may have figured in the end of the treason, it was not so in the beginning. He had already lost his faith in the One who called him to be an Apostle. The Gospel says that he was already "a devil."

2. *Social veneering.* Conscience is a peculiar thing. When a man loses his sense of individual justice and the ties that bind him to God, he sometimes seeks to compensate for it by an apparent love of social justice. Separating the two Commandments of the love of God and the love of neighbor, he attempts to have a brotherhood of man without the Fatherhood of God—a process which would make us a race of illegitimate children, not knowing our Father. When those who betray America lose their faith, they generally develop an abnormal passion for what they call social justice, plead their love of the proletariat, protest against any display of luxury, particularly if associated with religion, and demand, "Why has all this money been spent on this church?" In their individual lives, they repudiate all morality and justice, but now they invoke it in their feigned love of the poor. It is not because they are lovers of the poor that they plead for them; it is rather because they are envious of the wealth of others or else because they wish to use the poor to bomb their way to proletariat thrones. No man is more dangerous than he who pleads for social justice and yet negates individual justice in his own life.

Social veneering took its original pattern from Judas and is seen very clearly on the occasion when Our Blessed Lord was invited to the home of Simon the Pharisee. As was the custom in those days, Our Blessed Lord was reclining at table with His feet extended on the couch. A woman entered at the far end of the room, advanced until she stood above His feet, then let fall upon those sandaled harbingers of peace a few tears, like the first warm drops of the summer rain. Bringing out from under her veil a vessel of precious ointment, she broke it and poured it upon the feet of the Divine Master. Judas by this time, having completely lost all sense of spiritual values, could not see the worth of anything unless it was under an auctioneer's hammer. He now pretended to be scandalized that this perfume had not been sold and used for social work: "Why should not this ointment have been sold? It would have fetched two hundred silver pieces and alms might have been given to the poor." The Gospel immediately adds, "He said this, not from any concern of the poor, but because he was a thief; he kept the common purse and took what was put in it."

Critics are often men who fail. Criticism is often the outcome of an incapacity to appreciate true values. Judas was now using the Communist technique of pleading love for the poor. His conscience, he prided himself, was clear, for he was foretelling Marx: "You have nothing to lose but your chains."

3. *Mask of patriotism.* When a man betrays his country and allies himself to the mouthings of "social justice," he must necessarily wear a mask. On the outside, he appears patriotic; on the inside, he belongs to the Communists. This mask of patriotism can be so carefully kept in place that not even his associates know that he is a traitor or a Communist. He may be in the Army, in a defense plant, in an atomic plant, in communications, radio, education, television, labor unions, or he may hold a high place in government. Those who work with him never suspect his disloyalty to his country; when there is an accusation made against him to that effect, there will be not wanting those in high positions who will come to court,

pleading, "This man is not a traitor." Not having spiritual discernment to see behind the mask, they take the appearance of patriotism for reality. When finally suspicion grows, proofs multiply, and the traitor is brought for questioning by his country, his reaction is one of anger that anyone should suspect his Americanism. As the unlawful woman in the courtroom of Solomon shouted more loudly for the child than the lawful mother, so the traitors are now more loud in their pretended love of the country than the loyal citizens. In their protests, they roar, "This is an inquisition, a persecution. How dare you ask if I be a loyal American! I am so loyal to my country and to the Bill of Rights, and particularly to the Fifth Amendment,

that I now take it, wrap it about me, that all of you may see how much I love the Constitution."

When there are rats in a house, those who dwell therein may quarrel among themselves as to the advisability of using a trap baited with Gorgonzola's putrid smell, or with the more gentle, ventilated variety of Swiss cheese. Though there be those who protest against Gorgonzola smelling up the house, and though they may justly plead for another kind of cheese, let them never forget the big problem, which is to rid the house of rats.

In the case of Judas the mask of loyalty was so skillfully worn that the other Apostles did not know he was a traitor. This was proved by the fact that when Our Blessed Lord said the night of the Last Supper, "One of you is about to betray Me," eleven men leaned forward, saying, "Is it I? Is it I? Is it I?" One man *pulled back* and said, "Is it I?" When one is falsely accused, he will advance toward the aggressor or the one who charges him wrongly; but when the charge is true, he will fall back, shrinking as it were from the truth of the accusation. It was this rapid retreat from the face of the Master that inspired artists in the painting of the Last Supper to picture Judas knocking over the salt. Our Blessed Lord in His infinite kindness sent Judas out into the night, but did it so quietly that the other Apostles thought that He was sending him on a mission of giving money to the poor.

A short time later Judas is leading a band of Roman soldiers over the Brook of Cedron. These men in the army of a foreign power would not know Our Blessed Lord, so they had to be given a sign. Holding up his lantern and turning toward them, Judas said, "He whom I shall kiss, that is He. Lay hold of Him." Judas then advances to Our Blessed Lord, throws his arms around His neck, and blisters His lips with a kiss. Divinity is always so sacred that it must be betrayed by some mark of external affection such as a kiss. The traitor wears the mask of patriotism; Judas offers the sign of affection. It was Judas who knew where to find Our Lord after dark. The greatest betrayals come from within, that is, from those who are cradled within the sacred associations of the Christian community.

Our Blessed Lord said to Judas, "Friend, wilt thou betray the Son of Man with a kiss?" Judas now tears off the mask—no more need of Fifth Amendment, no more need of a kiss. He belongs now to the forces of evil, where he believes that his hatred will be given a collective strength, thanks to which he will have a place high and mighty when the revolution comes.

4. *Disillusionment and despair.* When the traitor is unmasked and he surveys the rotted fruit of his disloyalty, he perceives how little he has gained. Fuchs in England received but little from the high priests of Communism. The Canadian spies had almost empty hands at the end of their betrayal. Some of the most famous American traitors received only traveling expenses for selling the country and rotting their own souls. When they are brought to trial, perhaps a few fellow travelers in their own lands will help defray their legal expenses, but the Communists do not lift a hand to help them. The Communist forces repudiate them as useless tools that served their day and now are fit only for the scrap heap of discarded fools. One of the punishments of concerted evil is mutual recrimination. The enemies whom they served so cheaply now not only deny them justice, but pity.

Conscience sometimes speaks in a whisper when it ought

to speak loudest. After its warnings have been repudiated, it becomes like a lamp that goes out or flickers in the thickest darkness. The traitor now begins to hate everything connected with his crime. The responsibility for it cannot be shaken off. Conscience now begins to reaffirm itself. One can stop the clock, but not the sunrise or the stirrings of a guilty soul. When in pursuit of an object through deceit, one can stifle conscience; but when the object is attained, what was a warning conscience before sin now becomes a knowing conscience after sin. First it was lulled; now it becomes the worm that dieth not.

When Judas was unmasked, he looked to see what he had —never before did thirty pieces of silver look so cheap. In our money it was about seventeen dollars and forty cents. Divinity and fatherland are always sold out of all proportions to their real worth. No longer wanting the effect of his sin because he has sold himself too cheaply, he now takes back the money, sends it rolling and jingling across the temple floor, as his knowing conscience bids him speak: "I have betrayed innocent blood." They had no more use for him than Moscow has for a Communist who betrays his country, as they said, "Look thou to it." There was nothing they could do with the money except to buy a field of blood. Judas repented not his crime, but merely the consequences of his crime. He repented to himself, not to the Lord, as some today would repent to a psychoanalyst, and not to their Saviour.

To hate self is self's slaughter. Judas takes a rope, wends his way out to the valley of death. The soft yellow clay which gives way so quickly under his feet is as a rock compared with his sinking and despairing soul. In the hardness of the stones, he sees his heart; in every branch of the lean trees, an accusing finger; every knot in the trunk was like an eye, reading judgment. He had only one thought in his mind, and that was to empty himself of himself. As he betrayed One Who united Heaven and earth, so now he would try to separate them. He throws a rope over the tree, hangs himself, and bursts asunder. He had emptied himself of himself. On the hill opposite was the One Who could have saved him.

One can sell Christ as Judas did, but one cannot buy Him; one can sell America, but one cannot buy America, because love is not for sale. Judas, however, in the end may have been nobler than some traitors of their country, for at least Judas acknowledged that he betrayed innocent blood; few traitors today ever admit betraying America. Traitors will cease in America when Americans recover their faith.

CHAPTER TWENTY-FOUR

Prayer

Happiness is conditioned upon the vision of a larger world. Hardly anything in this world lives by itself. Coal needs oxygen to burn; fish need water to swim; birds need the air to fly; plants are in communion with the sun, which is over 92 million miles away from the earth. Every animal organism demands the whole of nature as its complement. It is too obvious to need development to remind man that his sufficiency is not from himself. We are not creators of energy; we are transformers of energy. It is a simple lesson in dynamics that the power that we expend is due to the power that we take in from without. As Alexis Carrel has said, "All beings seek to augment finite strength by tapping infinite reservoirs of power." This contact is achieved by prayer. Nature is to the body what God is to the soul.

As the deaf are dead to the great environment of harmony and sound, such as the laughter of a child and the sigh of a waterfall; as the blind are dead to the environment of beauty, such as the first spring flower and the radiant glow of the sunset—so there are those who are Deity-blind. This condition they have imposed upon themselves as if they had plucked out their own eyes. Some call themselves humanists, boasting that they can lift themselves by their own bootstraps or be healthy by breathing in the same air they breathe out. Others are atheists, who have well been defined as those "who have no invisible means of support." Human nature has the unfortunate tendency often to depreciate what is unknown, such as a love of poetry or good music. One of the reasons why many are unhappy in this world is because the body is going too fast for the soul.

The great difference between the contact of lower creation with nature, and the contact of the soul with God is that the first is automatic and the second is free. Respiration, digestion, circulation, vision are reflex actions. It is harder to hold the breath than to breathe. This suggests that some positive effort of restraint is made to shut out an environment which is helpful to our well-being.

At any moment of our lives there are floating round in our environment sound waves bearing music, comedy, political discussions, operas, and other radio programs. In like manner, the Divine energy of peace and joy is floating through this world, but many are not receiving it because they chose not to tune in by an act of the will. Millions and millions of favors are hanging from heaven on silken cords, and prayer is the sword that cuts them.

The painting of Holman Hunt represents Our Blessed Lord knocking at an ivy-covered door with a lantern in His hand. Holman Hunt was criticized on the ground that he had no latch on the outside of the door. His answer was, "Of course not. The latch is on the inside. We alone can open it." It is for free men to accept or reject the favors and blessings of God. Man must *will* to receive. Prayer is an opportunity to let in what would otherwise be left out. Air is there if we breathe, light is there if we open our eyes, and the gifts we receive from heaven depend on our trust. Prayer opens possibilities. House plants cannot live without water; the flowers will give us their blossoms only if we give them water. Windows will let in light, if we clean them. Our hearts will let in God, if we purify them. Blessings come to those who put themselves in an environment of love.

Here is an orphaned, homeless child of the street. This other little girl is in a very happy home. She has all she needs for her happiness, such as food, clothing, shelter, and affection. The first child has none of these blessings because she is devoid of the environment of love. The homeless child outside that environment lacks those advantages. In like manner, those who do not through prayer place themselves in this environment of Divine Love and Power miss the graces and happiness which others enjoy. Some parents refuse to raise a family, saying, "I could not afford to send my child to college." Obviously their only resources are the bank account. If, however, they put themselves in the environment of Divine Love, trusting in God Who made them, then they would receive the prosperity which presently they are denied. We do not trust those who do not trust us. Just as soon as we trust others, they open their hearts to us. So it is with the Lord.

Distractions should not be a serious problem in prayer. St. Bernard had a friend once who told him he never had any distractions. St. Bernard confessed to having trouble with them. The two were out horseback riding when St. Bernard said, "I will give you this horse, if you can say the Our Father without distraction. Now, get off your horse and say the Our Father." His friend got as far as the words, "Give us this day our daily bread," when he looked up at St. Bernard and asked, "Can I have the saddle too?"

A sick man who was brought to a hospital said to the good nun in charge, "I haven't prayed in thirty years. Pray for me." She said, "Pray for yourself. Sometimes the strange voice is the one most quickly heard."

Prayer may be briefly treated under the three titles of petition, worship, and action.

In petitionary prayer we do not tell God our needs, for

He knows those before we begin. Rather we give Him an opportunity to bestow them on us. Prayer is helplessness casting itself on Power, infirmity leaning on Strength, misery reaching to Mercy, and a prisoner clamoring for Relief.

God has two kinds of gifts—those He gives us whether we pray or not, and those He gives us on condition we put ourselves in the area of His Love. God may want to give us something but cannot, because our hands are full of tinsel. Many regard God as an aviator regards a parachute. They hope they never need Him, but if they do, He may come in handy.

Prayer does not change God's will, but it may change ours, that we become receptive to His blessings. A father wishes to send his son to college. During high-school days the boy becomes recalcitrant and disobedient, steals, has a police record, and becomes a juvenile delinquent. He is finally sent to reform school. Has the father changed his will about sending him to college? The father still wills it, but the boy does not go to college even though the father wills it. It is because the boy has not fulfilled those conditions which were necessary for the father's giving him a college education. Prayer, in like manner, is the fulfillment of conditions which make greater blessings possible.

Normally, priests are ordained at the age of twenty-four. I was ordained at twenty-four, but evidently must have been mentally retarded for I was sent to universities for five more years. Five years after my ordination, I was studying philosophy at the University of Louvain in Belgium. I wished to go to Lourdes to celebrate the fifth anniversary of my priesthood.

Lourdes is known not only to the faithful, but to almost everyone through the movie, *The Song of Bernadette*, and Franz Werfel's book on the same subject. I had enough money to go to Lourdes, but not enough to live on once I arrived. I asked my brother, who was studying medicine at the University of Louvain, for some money. He was a typical university student, too. I reflected, "Well, if I have faith enough to go to Lourdes to celebrate the fifth anniversary of my ordination, it is up to the Blessed Mother to get me out." I went to Lourdes and arrived broke. I then figured that if the Blessed Mother would pay my hotel bill, she could just as well pay a big one as a little one. I went to the best hotel in Lourdes. It was fourth-rate by our standards, but it was the best hotel in Lourdes. On the fifth day I received my bill. I had visions of gendarmes and jails, but I stuck it out because the novena called for nine days of prayer. I went down to the shrine on the morning of the ninth day. Nothing happened. The ninth noon nothing happened. The ninth evening nothing happened—then it was serious. I decided to give the Blessed Mother another chance. I paid a visit to the shrine about half-past ten that night. As I was saying the rosary, a portly gentleman tapped me on the shoulder. "Are you an American priest? Do you speak French? Do you know Paris? Well, I am Mr. —— from New York. This is my son and my daughter and my wife." We walked back to the hotel together. "We want you to come to Paris with us tomorrow and talk French for us." He said, "Have you paid your hotel bill yet?" That was the most interesting question I have ever heard in my life. I outfumbled him for the bill. It was one of those not too rare moments in life where the grasp does not exceed the reach. We went to Paris, stayed there for a week, at the end of which he said, "I will give you my address in New York. Do you mind taking it at the bottom of a check?" "Not particularly," I answered. I arrived back at Louvain with much more than I started with. We have since returned to Lourdes two times together to thank the Blessed Mother for introducing us one to another.

The moral of this story is not to go to the Waldorf-Astoria and expect the Blessed Mother to pay your bill; the moral is that the Heavenly Mother does intercede to Her Divine Son for importunate and demanding children.

In addition to petition, there is also worship. It has been asked, "Why does God want praise? Is He a potentate, sitting on a throne, very unhappy and miserable when we do not pay Him some adulation?"

God does not need praise; we need to give it. In many homes at springtime, little girls about three and four years of age go out to the lawn and gather up bunches of dandelions. The mother is presented with them very solemnly. This creates a difficulty. She must get a vase for the dandelions; she may even have to display them, which she certainly does not want to do.

The mother does not need the dandelions. But the child needs to give them. By accepting the dandelions, mother is training the child in love, kindness, and goodness. Not to give a gift to the mother, however humble the gift, would mean the child was wanting in affection and obedience. God does not need our praise; we need to give it.

Worship disaffects the soul of its prepossessions and attachments; de-egotizes it, creates a void such as is in a reed, which makes music possible. It prepares the soul for the reception of novelty, puts the ego out of self that the Divine may find a place. Detachment from self is always the condition of attachment to others. God pretends to need us, but we really need him for our perfection.

Worship, too, is praise. Unbelief is the enemy of praise; so is selfishness. Some think that, by praising others, they belittle themselves. As praise of God decreases, so encouragement of others decreases. We can no more do anything to diminish the glory of God than a lunatic can blot out the sun by writing "darkness" on the wall of a cave.

How little we praise our fellow man! Does a husband ever thank a wife for preparing meals? In eighteen years she has prepared over 19,000 meals. Does a wife ever praise a husband for supporting her? Where there is love, there is gratitude and praise.

A brief word about prayer as action. All work can be turned into prayer as can all play, recreation, sorrow, and contradiction. Those who work booms and cameras in television studios, stenographers, taxi drivers, bartenders, doctors, housekeepers, ballplayers—all can turn their work into prayer provided they offer it in the name of the Good Lord.

Down in the gutter of a city street was a drop of water,

soiled, dirty, and stagnant. Way up in the heavens, a gentle sunbeam saw it; leaped from out of the azure sky, down to the drop, kissed it, thrilled it through and through with new strange life and hopes, lifted it up higher and higher and higher beyond the clouds, and one day left it as a flake of immaculate snow on a mountaintop. So our own humdrum, routine, workaday lives in the pantry and in the school, in the office and on the farm, in the machine shop can be ennobled, spiritualized, and divinized, provided we bring to them the inspiration of Someone who saw apostolic zeal in salt; provided we bring to them the inspiration of a Captain bearing five wounds in the forefront of battle; provided we bring to them the fixed flash of that instant and intolerant Enlightenment—the Lightning made eternal as the Light.

CHAPTER TWENTY-FIVE

Brain Washing

One of the most diabolical practices the world has ever known, which today is universal throughout the Communist world, is the phenomenon of brain washing. It may be interesting to explain:

1. The psychology behind it.
2. The nature of brain washing and brain changing.
3. Its effects on the mind.

Origin. The science of psychology for centuries was rightly concerned with the higher nature of man, who is properly defined as a rational animal. Recently, the rational aspect of man has been neglected, as psychology starts with the assumption that man is like an animal. Therefore, the proper study of man is his reflexes. Reflexes are of two kinds: unconditioned and conditioned. We are all very familiar with reflexes. A wink is an unconditioned reflex. It takes a man only a second to give a wink, but it may take a lifetime to undo it. Claude Bernard brought to a scientific level a phenomenon known to everyone, namely, how the mouths of dogs water when meat is put before them. I once had a dog. If I put meat before his eyes and said, "Lent," he would not touch it. Not until I said "Easter" would he touch the meat. This was a conditioned reflex.

Ivan Petrovich Pavlov, a Russian who in 1904 received the Nobel prize in medicine, specialized in the psychology of conditioned reflexes. Every time he gave a dog food, he rang a bell. His intent was to superimpose upon the brain a conditioned reflex, namely, salivation of the mouth when the bell rang. The bell was rung hundreds and hundreds of times when the dog was fed. After several months, Dr. Pavlov did not give the dog any food, but just rang the bell, and the dog's mouth watered. That was what was known as a conditional reflex. That is to say, he was conditioned mechanically and automatically to react to a certain stimulus.

Starting with the assumption that man is an animal, he concluded falsely that all psychic activity in man is begotten of the same mechanical stimulus and response. The conditioned reflex (salivation at the sound of the bell) was grafted onto the necessary reaction (salivation at the presence of food). So man, it was believed, could have conditional reflexes grafted on his normal thought processes. Though he did not develop the idea, Pavlov implied that "suggestion" was the simplest way to create a conditioned reflex in man.

Hypnotism is the use of verbal reflexes; for example, certain words suggest sleep to the patient, others cold. Hence speech, propaganda and repetition are the best forms of artificially conditioning a human mind to react in a certain way. A phrase used to describe the breakup of the mind or a complete loosening of morals is, "The man has gone to the dogs." Pavlov "went to the dogs," and the Communists have given man a "dog's life" ever since.

Another Russian, by the name of V. V. Bechterev, said, "The word plays the role of an external stimulus and becomes a substitute, according to the association established, for an external influence, on a certain inner state." As in hypnotism words act as triggers on the brain, so in waking life the external suggestions are thought to take the place of internal decisions. The mind will respond automatically to what is suggested. Thus inside motivation of the will and the inner decision of the spirit are abandoned in favor of a suggestion from the outside that belongs to the animal or mechanical order.

This psychology, as developed by the Soviets, produced what is known as brain washing and brain changing.

Nature of brain washing and brain changing. Brain washing seeks to cleanse the mind of its former ideas; the pouring in of Communist ideas is called brain changing, or indoctrination. The normal man must be made abnormal; the higher and nobler part of man must be washed away. The slate must be cleaned, before the Communists can write on it. This figure represents man who thinks and who wills according to his God-given faculties.

The Communists seek to *obliterate*, *destroy*, and *eradicate* all that makes man a man. If an image could represent it, this is brain washing:

The less reasonable a man is, the more likely he is to become a Communist. Hence his ideas of justice, goodness, love of neighbor, family must all be washed away to make room for hate, knavery, lying, and deceit, which Lenin said were essential for making the revolution. The less rational a man is, the more susceptible he is to external impressions and suggestions, as is, for example, an idiot.

But how destroy conscience and reason so that the subconscious is made available to outside influences? The Communists use various ways of washing the brain. One way is by injection. That method was tried on Cardinal Mindszenty by a Hungarian psychiatrist who had spent two years studying the cruel methods of the Soviets. Over the unconscious body of Mindszenty, the doctor said to his associates, "Out of this particular vial here, I can make him a gigolo; out of this vial, a Communist. We will bring him before the people; he will look exactly as he looked before, but he will have a new brain

—he will have a Soviet soul." The injection failed. The psychiatrist became angry and shouted, "Why is it that Jesus was able to drive the devil out of a man, and I can't put the devil into a man?"

Along with this method of brain changing there are also the torture cells devised by the Communists (see photograph facing page 224).

The two ledges at the sides suggest beds for rest, but the slanting position makes it impossible for anyone to rest on them. The paint is red, to suggest the blood Communists spill. The bricks fastened to the floor make it impossible for a person to sit, or even stand at ease. The conflicting lines on the right wall suggest the dead-end streets of the mind, with no possible outlet or escape. The checkered board on the wall is a reminder of the fictitious bars of a prison, which suggest light, but admit none. The spots on the wall are to arrest attention, so as to keep the mind from wandering from this red inferno. The Communists sometimes put a solution in the eyes which makes it impossible to close them; one has to fix his gaze upon these crazy patterns until he goes insane. The Communists found after they used these torture chambers that they could drive people mad by making them stand for days and nights before a blazing light.

In China, the Communists have developed a new method. It is not based on incessant violence, though some violence is used. Rather, the principle is to break down the mind through fatigue. The prisoner is given powdered rice but is not allowed to drink until five hours after consuming the powdered rice.

He therefore eats less and less because his mouth is so dry. Furthermore, he is permitted to satisfy the needs of nature only after long periods of time. When arrested, he is kept standing before a blazing light for seventy hours or more. Then he is told he may sleep. The prisoner sleeps for fifteen minutes, then is kept awake for eight hours; is told to sleep again, but is awakened after thirty minutes, and kept awake for six hours. This goes on for months, and with this constant interrogation during night trials the mind becomes so fatigued that memory is gone. A missionary stated that after such an ordeal she could not remember a single word of the English language, though she was an American. Another missionary, a Frenchman, said that all he could remember was the first three words of the *Hail Mary*. Two hundred and thirty-six Polish priests, when Russia seized Poland, were marched toward Afghanistan; only two after extreme torture could remember the *Our Father*.

The purpose of the light is to tire the optic centers so much that they cease to react to outer stimulation. The mind is thus unable to function well when deprived, through fatigue, of outer stimuli. The aim is to distract the mind from having many thoughts, so that it cannot find repose within. The light and the fatigue aid in forcing concentration so that it becomes more automatic and conditioned to Communist suggestions.

All the while, during the incessant questionings, the Communist judges sit for four hours each, but the prisoner stands night after night. He is charged with being an imperialist spy, with helping to spread germ warfare, and with murdering infants. False evidence is presented, as the prisoner is shouted

down by Communist mobs. The mind is exhausted, the will weakened; one is isolated, told that friends have betrayed, that others confessed to his guilt. When the rational nature of man is tortured to a point where it barely functions, the Communists are ready for brain washing, or indoctrination, or the producing of automatic reactions and conditioned reflexes.

When old ideas are "wiped away," new ideas are put in their place. In sleep, the body goes into dry dock for repairs. When the sleep is natural, we are *en rapport* with our consciousness. In hypnosis and after great fatigue, the mind is more *en rapport* with the outside world. The level of volition and the threshold of consciousness are lowered. Outside suggestions now become the dictators of nervous energy. One is now told to make a "confession" of his "evil," which means any thoughts, words, or deeds against Communism. When one confesses to being a "spy" in China, the process is called *Tai-mao-tsu*, or "putting on the hat" of an imperialist.

Loud-speakers blare out Communist ideas, prison guards repeat Communist phrases as they march before the cell; the prisoner is forced to face a wall, and write out for hours, without stopping, Communist ideas. The plan is to have these ideas filter into the mind, in the fond hope that just as soon as these ideas are repeated again, then, like the dog with the bell, one will automatically react in Communist fashion.

Imagine a man losing his rational soul, so that he just had a lifeless body left. Then picture the life principle of a snake coming into the body. From that time on, the man could no longer speak, think, love, produce, know science, or do anything human—though he would look like a human. The Communist principle of indoctrination is just that, save that the Communists seek to put the devil inside a man.

The God-given image is destroyed, and the image of the devil is set up in its place. The world is turned upside down, virtue is eliminated, vice takes its place. Honor is gone, disloyalty becomes honor; honesty becomes dishonesty; love becomes hate; night becomes day; day becomes night. Never before has the world seen the philosophy of distortion practiced on such a universal scale. The Gospel mentions many cases of individual possessions by the devil; today there is collective possession, which is sometimes called Communism.

One of our missionaries in Manchuria, after being kept six months in prison, was told by the judges, "Say it is raining outside. Say it a hundred times, say it a thousand times." He did. Then after a thousand times they interjected the line, "America is an imperialist country." He said, "I refuse." They said, "Say 'It's raining outside.'" He refused. Four hours later he found himself standing, half conscious, saying, "America is an imperialist country." They had succeeded, at least for the moment, in creating a conditioned reflex.

The test given by the Communists, whereby they know whether one is indoctrinated, is to beat fellow prisoners. A guard said to one of our friends in China, "Take this iron rod and beat the other prisoners." She refused. He said, "You are not convinced. Your brain has not been changed." "How do you know?" she asked. "Because you don't hate."

The effect of brain washing. The effect of imprisonment,

isolation, torture, persecution, brain washing, and propaganda is to create a conflict within the mind. One second the mind seems to say, "What they say is true"; the next second, "It is not true." One moment it believes the propaganda, but the next moment it denies it. In cases of great fatigue and exhaustion, the prisoner may really believe that he is telling the truth when he makes a "confession" such as the Communists tell him to make. A Presbyterian minister, the Reverend John D. Hayes, a Rhodes scholar, was subjected in China to forty days of inquiry, about nine hours each day. He said he felt no longer like a person or a citizen, but like an automaton. He finally began to see the fabrications, for, as he put it, "A trained mind cannot hold things separate which are relatable."

Does the effect of brain washing endure? Generally not. A path can be made through a forest, but vegetation will soon cover it up. The Divine image in the soul may be blurred by Communist technique, but it can be restored.

An American in the Embassy at Moscow was arrested by the Soviets, who wanted to get rid of him. The charge was rape. They kept him in prison, tortured, and brain-washed him. After three months he "confessed" his guilt. His fellow Americans at the Embassy asked, "Why did you confess?" He answered, "Because they had the goods on me." He came back to America. His senses, his intellect, and his will began to function properly. In the meantime, the American Embassy in Moscow made an investigation. They found the young man was not in Moscow the day of the alleged crime. He was in another city that day, but at the time he really believed he was guilty.

The Soviets have proved to the world the awful and frightening consequence of treating man as an animal. Let democracy be careful that it does not teach the same lesson. Brain washing in jail is vicious, but there can be brain washing in our schools if we teach that man is no different from the beast. Democracy will be preserved only by teaching the dignity of the human person; a person has dignity and rights only because, as our Declaration of Independence states, he has been endowed with these by God. May our educators never wash our brains of true Americanism!

CHAPTER TWENTY-SIX

Three Times in a Nation's History

Our Blessed Lord once chided men for not understanding the times in which they lived; as the Pharisees and Sadducees came and put him to the test, asking him to show them a sign from heaven, He answered them, "When evening comes, you say, It is fair weather, the sky is red; or at sun-rise, There will be a storm to-day, the sky is red and lowering. You know, then, how to read the face of heaven; can you not read the signs of appointed times?"

One reason why many do not understand the times in which they live is because they are so much immersed in the succession of events; judging today by yesterday and tomorrow by today, they completely lack a standard by which the times may be evaluated. When the hand is too close to the eye, the latter cannot see the distant horizon; when minds are too close to events, they cannot understand their meaning. As a clock must be set by a standard of time outside the clock itself, as cloth must be measured by a ruler outside of the cloth, so man must judge his times by other standards than the political and the economic in which he lives.

One day this Great Patriot looked over the city and civilization in which He lived; foreseeing the doom it was about to bring upon itself, He wept tears of sorrow. "Ah, if thou too couldst understand, above all in this day that is granted thee, the ways that can bring thee peace! As it is, they are hidden from thy sight. The days will come upon thee when thy enemies will fence thee round about, and encircle thee, and press thee hard on every side, and bring down in ruin both thee and thy children that are in thee, not leaving one stone of thee upon another; and all because thou didst not recognize the time of my visiting thee."

According to this statement, every civilization has three moments:

1. A time of privilege, in which there is a visitation of God's grace.
2. A time of blindness, when truths begin to be hidden from sight.
3. A time of judgment, when the evil men do produces heinous effects.

Western civilization had its time of visitation, when, enriched by the great Christian tradition, stones began crying out in Gothic cathedrals, education disciplined the mind until it was ready to produce the beginnings of modern science, and law developed the doctrine of the inviolability and eternal worth of human personality.

The time of national blindness came at the end of World

War II. During that war there were three evil philosophies of Communism, Nazism, and Fascism. The only difference between the three was the difference between murder, killing, and taking a life. All three were alike in the destruction of human personality; the difference was the way in which personality was destroyed. Communism absorbed a man into the class, Nazism into the race, and Fascism into the state. But, in our moment of blindness, the Western world said, "Only two of these philosophies are evil; one is good and is to be labeled a democracy, namely, Communism."

Visitation, blindness, and finally judgment. Judgment does not mean that God strikes us in wrath; it is rather that He allows us to punish ourselves for our own misdeeds. He made nature a certain way; when we disobey nature's laws, we suffer the consequences; these consequences are the registering of judgment. For example, it is a law of nature that we eat; if we do not eat, we suffer a headache. A headache is a judgment upon our violation of the law of nature. It is a law of reason that we should study; if we do not study, we become ignorant. Ignorance can, therefore, be a judgment on our failure to make use of educational opportunities. If we disobey the moral laws of God, we produce certain catastrophic effects such as wars and revolutions. Some civilizations reach such a stage of aberration and decay that God can show His pity only by cracking them like an egg.

Nature is on God's side, not ours. This is what is meant by its "traitorous trueness, its loyal deceit"; it will be fickle to us,

turn against us and betray us, unless we use it in the ways appointed by God. If one could graph what is taking place in the
world, it might be as follows:

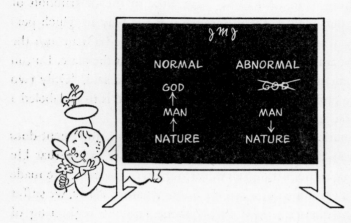

Nature was meant to serve man; man was meant to evolve
and develop into union with Perfect Love through the assistance of that Merciful Love.

An unhealthy condition for man and society arises when
man neglects that which is his perfection and happiness and
goes down to what is below him in dignity, such as nature,
animal sensualism, material values, or crass materialism. When
man descends to the level of the material, and identifies his goal
of life with it, nature rebels against him. For example, alcohol
says to man, "I am your servant; I was made to minister to your
feasts, and to gladden your heart. But you have refused to be
my master by using me intemperately and irrationally. Now,

in revenge, I shall turn against you and enslave you. From now
on, you will be an alcoholic."

A visitor to the Louvre, after looking at the masterpieces of
painting for an hour, became exasperated and said to the guide,
"There is not a thing in here worth looking at. Too many
Madonnas, too many pictures of Christ." The guide answered,
"Sir! These pictures are not on trial; you are." A civilization,
in like manner, that rejects the Divine, chooses material values
as the final goal of life, does not put theology or right reason
on trial; it puts itself on trial. It is already judged.

If modern man has chosen secularism in the Western world
and Dialectical Materialism in Russia, what would be a fitting
judgment for our times? Obviously matter itself. Could it be
that our identification with the material should be the source of
our disintegration? And what part of matter? Obviously that
which is lowest in matter, the primate of all chemicals; namely,
an atom of hydrogen which becomes a bomb. Minds today
have a passion for fission and analysis, instead of for unity and
synthesis. Having fissioned our minds, maybe this primal thing
in all nature may turn against us, revolt against us, and become
our judgment! That would be a hydrogen blast which might
bring harm to the planet itself.

Pius XII, addressing the Pontifical Academy of Science, two
years before the atom bomb exploded over Hiroshima, gave
the exact explosive power of atomic energy. He then pleaded
with the nations that "such energy never be used destruc-
tively"; he warned that it would bring great harm to those

places where it was used, and eventually to the planet itself.

It is well to recall the words of Goncourt, the French publisher, on the occasion of a visit from Claude Bernard and René Berthelot, two distinguished scientists of France. They explained to Goncourt the destructive power hidden in chemistry and said that science had just begun to lisp the alphabet of destruction. The full measure of science's power for annihilation would be left to the twentieth century. Upon hearing this, Goncourt observed, "When that day comes, I believe that Almighty God will come down from the heavens like a night watchman rattling his keys, saying, 'Gentlemen, it's closing time'; then we will have to start all over again."

There is nothing to fear about hydrogen energy. God lights the sun with atomic energy. Atomic energy is just as harmless as a match. No man is fearful of a match when handed it by his neighbor. But when the match is in the hands of an arsonist, there is fear.

Atomic energy is a blessing, just like fire. Our worry is atomic men. Atomic men are those who identify themselves with the world and who believe man has no other destiny than the beast. Soon they discover that the world's rewards are not equal to the world's pains. As a man might hate a woman because she has not given to him all the pleasure he expected and all the heaven that she promised, so atomic men, finding that the world has betrayed them because they betrayed its Maker, now, feeling cheated, prepare to destroy it. If some atomic men have betrayed their country, after betraying their God, why would they not, in final despair, betray even the world and blow it to bits?

Why do we ask, "Must we die?" If we were quadrupeds, that would be a valid question. But, being men, we ought to ask, "Must we be reborn?" Must we change our home life, our vision of the world, change the way we educate our children that they may be brought up in fear of God and love of their parents? This emphasis makes us see that what we have to fear is not Russia, but our own guilt. Everyone in the world is guilty; everyone—ourselves, as well as Russia.

When the blood stream is infected with poison, it does no good to amputate an arm or a leg; there is not sufficient localization of evil to believe that the whole organism can be cured by war against one member. The whole world is sick today; "we all stand in need of redemption." No one wants Russia destroyed, no one wants America destroyed. There are too many good people in Russia and too many good people in America. If we saw the international problem clearly, we would see that we are defending a half truth against a lie. The Western world's half truth is defending a liberty that does not always recognize a law. The lie of Russia is defending a dictated law without liberty. Our half truth is insisting on rights without duties; their lie is insisting on slave duties without rights.

If the cause of the world's confusion were wholly outside ourselves, then we would be hopeless, for there would be nothing we could do to better it. But if the fault is not in the stars, or in determined historical processes, but in our hearts, then with God's help the whole world can be renewed through the renewal of ourselves. Salvation from world evil is possible only when everyone admits to the guilt for everything. The evil of Communist Russia is partly of our making, for the philosophy of Communism came from the Western world. Our trust must not, therefore, be put in self-righteous attitudes fringed about with weapons.

It may be well to look at the great battle that took place between the mastermind of evil, Goliath, and that Jewish shepherd boy who later on became King David. The giant Goliath was panoplied in armor from head to foot. King Saul of the Jews put his armor upon David and bade him go out to meet Goliath. David took it off; he could not walk in it. He said, "No, I shall go forth to meet Goliath in the name of the Lord of Hosts."

He went to a tree, cut from it a crotch, and made it into a slingshot; then, from a brook, he picked up five stones. Armed with that crossbar of wood and those five stones, he went out to meet Goliath. Goliath sneered at him and said to him, "Who do you think I am—a dog—that thou shouldst thus come to do battle with me?" David shot a stone, hit the only unprotected part of the body of Goliath, his forehead, and Goliath fell dead.

Goliath was destroyed in the moment of his greatest strength. Saul was the embodiment of worldly wisdom and calculating prudence. David was merely a prefiguration of Our Divine Saviour, Who met the forces of evil with the cross that looked like the slingshot of David. He took, not five stones from a rippling brook, but five wounds from rippling rivers of blood, and with these He conquered the Goliath of evil.

Nothing can ever happen in the world when evil will seem more powerful than it did the day Christ died on the Cross. And yet evil that slew the foe lost the war on Resurrection Day. Evil may have its hour, but God has His day. Our Christian faith always expects the unexpected; it is never defeated when things go wrong; it suits all the secret irregularities and all the dark hours of mechanized evil. Born in catastrophe, it knows how to meet it in Him Who is our Way, our Truth, and our Life.

Let America love its stars and stripes! But let it also realize that America will conquer by other stars and other stripes than those on our flag, namely, by the stars and stripes of Christ, by Whose stars we are illumined and by Whose stripes we are healed. We pray, too, that His Mother, who stood at the foot of the Cross, may intercede to her Divine Son, that our world may receive Him before it lies in ruins. "If God is with us, who can be against us?"